Tea Time Mini Coloring Book

40 Delightful Designs

for coloring in.

By Artist
Dwyanna Stoltzfus

Copyright © 2017 by Dwyanna Stoltzfus

ALL RIGHTS RESERVED

ISBN-10: 1976560780

13:978-1976560781

This publication is for personal use only.
No part of this publication may be reproduced, stored in a retrieval
System, or transmitted in any form or by any means – electronic, mechanical, photocopy,
Or any other - without the written permission
of the artist/publisher – Dwyanna Stoltzfus.

Unauthorized reproduction of any part of this publication by any means
Is an infringement of copyright.
All artwork and images in this publication are
Protected by copyright laws.

Join the Fun!!

Share your colored pages!!

You are invited to color the pages

From this and all publications by

Dwyanna Stoltzfus. Then scan and post

Your colored creations in

Coloring with Dwyanna

Adult Coloring Group

On facebook

https://web.facebook.com/groups/1519357628356169/?_rdr

Join Coloring with Dwyanna Coloring Group,

And have fun sharing your colored pages

And meeting new coloring friends.

Members of the group will also have access

To free coloring pages.

You are welcome to share your colored pages on

Any social network, make sure to mention the title of

The book and the author/artist name.

Uncolored images may not be shared.

Check out my blog at:

coloringwithdwyanna.blogspot.com

PDF Printable coloring pages available

On Etsy at

https://www.etsy.com/people/dwyannastoltzfus

Follow Dwyanna's art on facebook at

Oodles of Doodles Designs –

Adult Coloring Books by

Dwyanna Stoltzfus

https://web.facebook.com/Oodles-of-Doodles-Designs-Adult-Coloring-Books-by-Dwyanna-Stoltzfus-743502922387046/

About:

Get ready to color 40 delightful designs by Artist Dwyanna Stoltzfus.

At 6X9 inches this mini coloring book is the perfect size to take along wherever you go!!

In this adult coloring book you will find 40 beautiful illustrations, printed one per page.

A collection of wonderful images including tea pot, teacups, teddy bears,

A wonderful coo coo clock,

Sweets, flowers and more!!

You can use this coloring book to help you relax and unwind after a long day.

Or you can use it just for fun. You can color the designs simply or add depth

and creativity by shading and highlighting.

Crayons are not recommended for the intricate designs but may be used on some of the pages.

You can also color with fine tip markers, gel pens, and colored pencils.

Enjoy the experience of coloring!!

But most of all relax and have fun!!

Coloring tips:

If you desire to add depth to your coloring you can shade with colored pencils.

Use dark colors around edges and into the peaks. Blend in light colors for the

middle and more open spaces. You can use black to darken areas,

and white to lighten and brighten areas.

Acknowledgments

Thank You to my family for all your support

of my art and this project.

I could not have done it without you!!

Thank You God for the gift and love

Of art and drawing!!

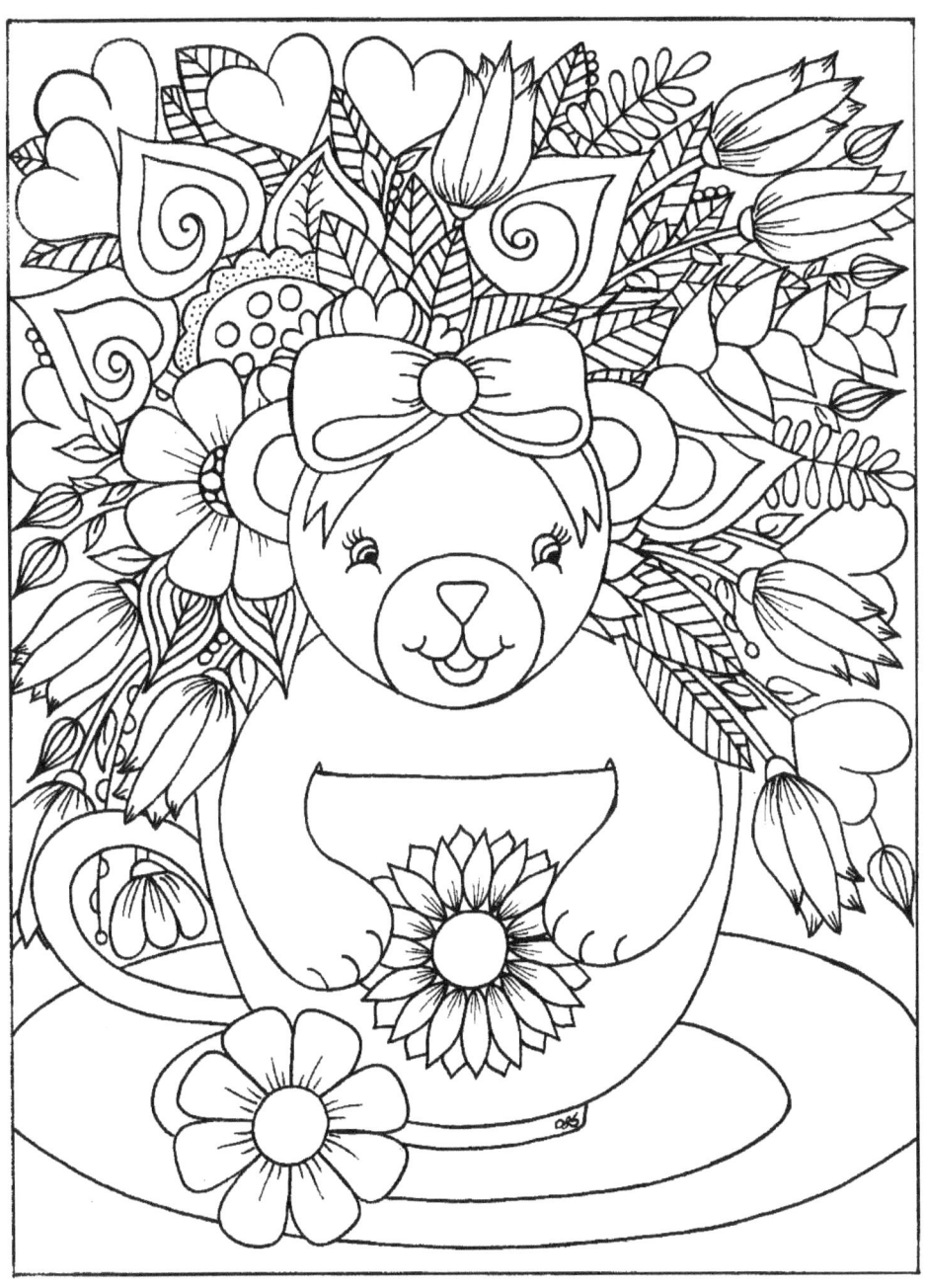

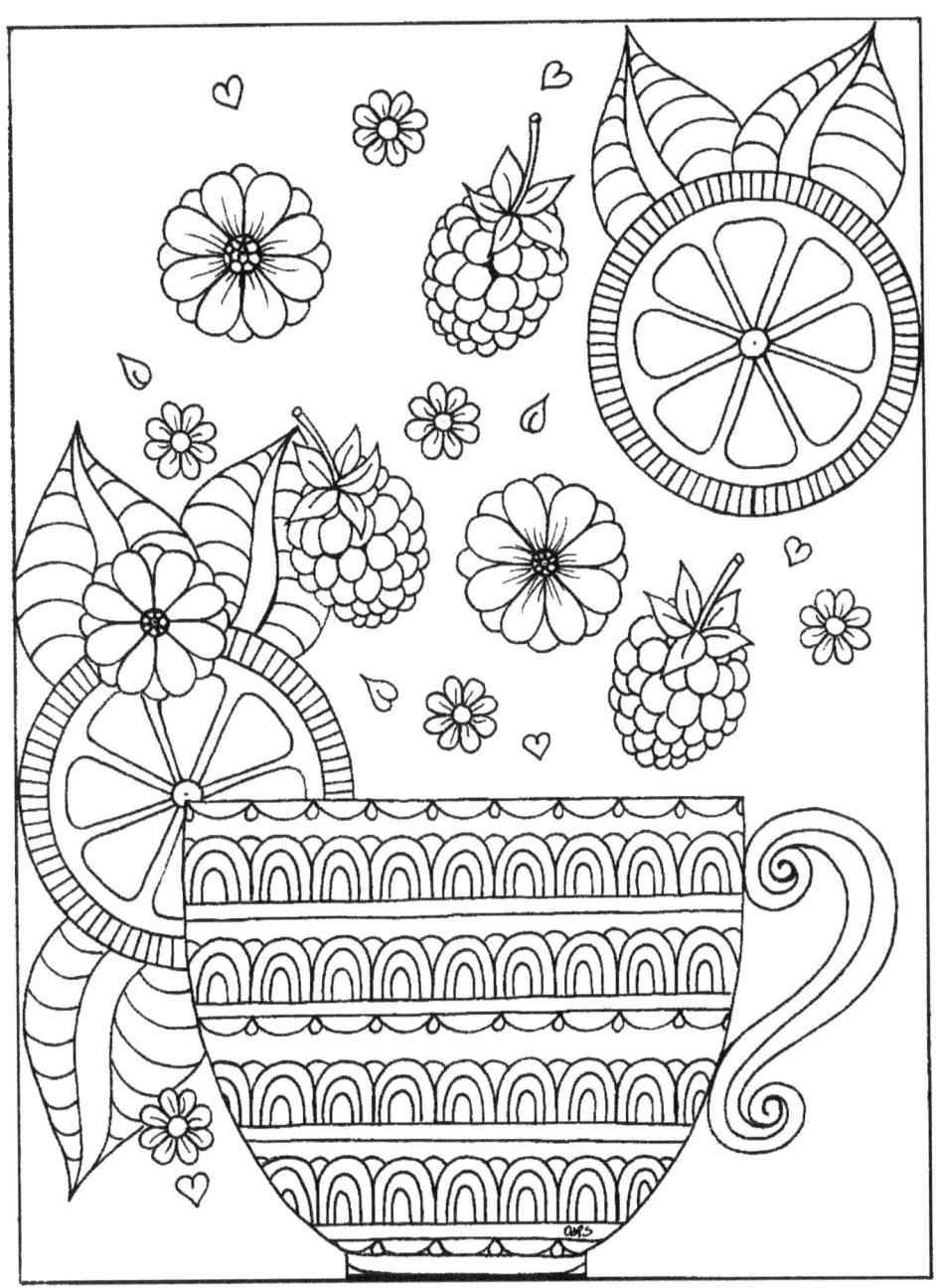

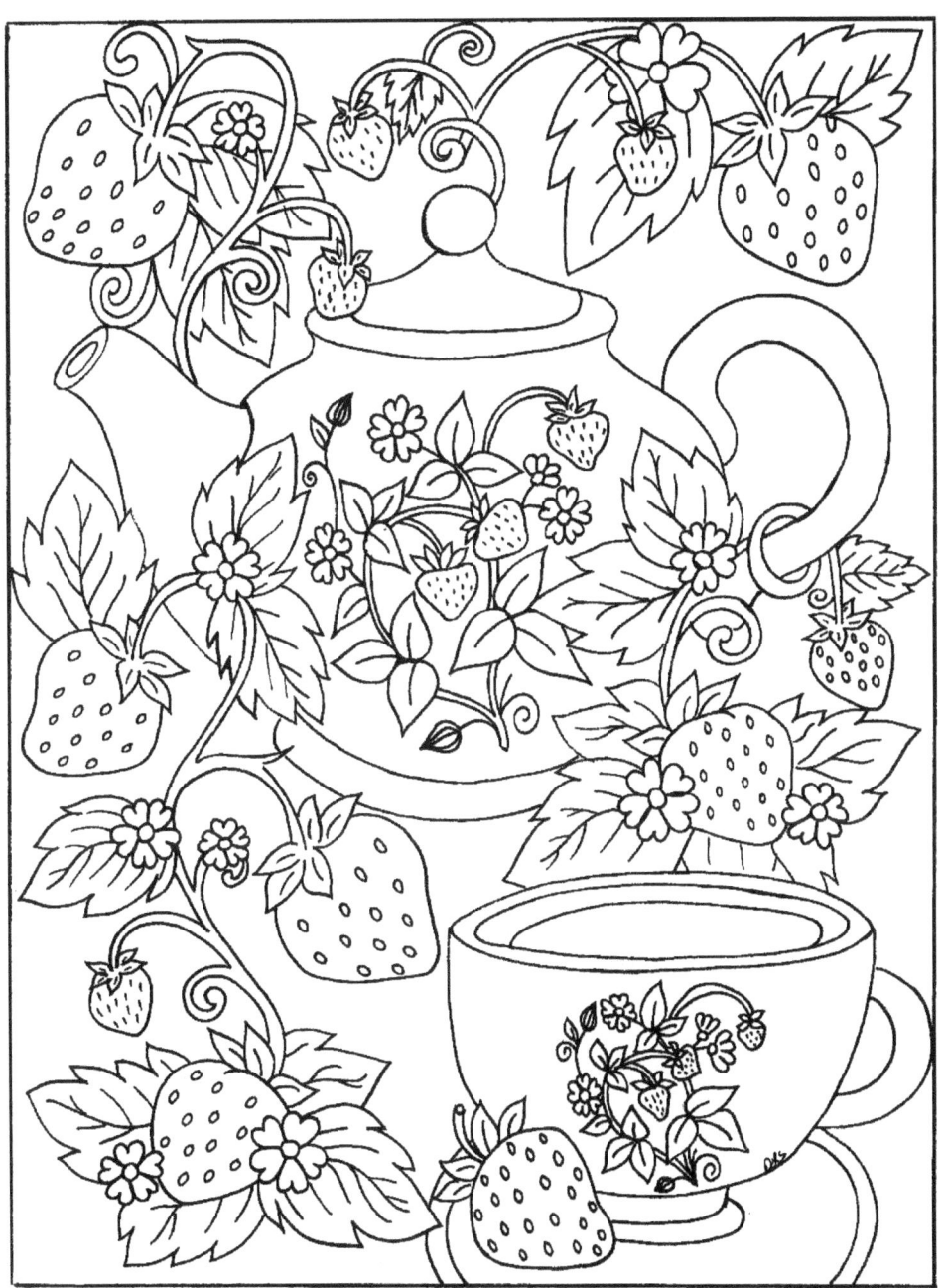

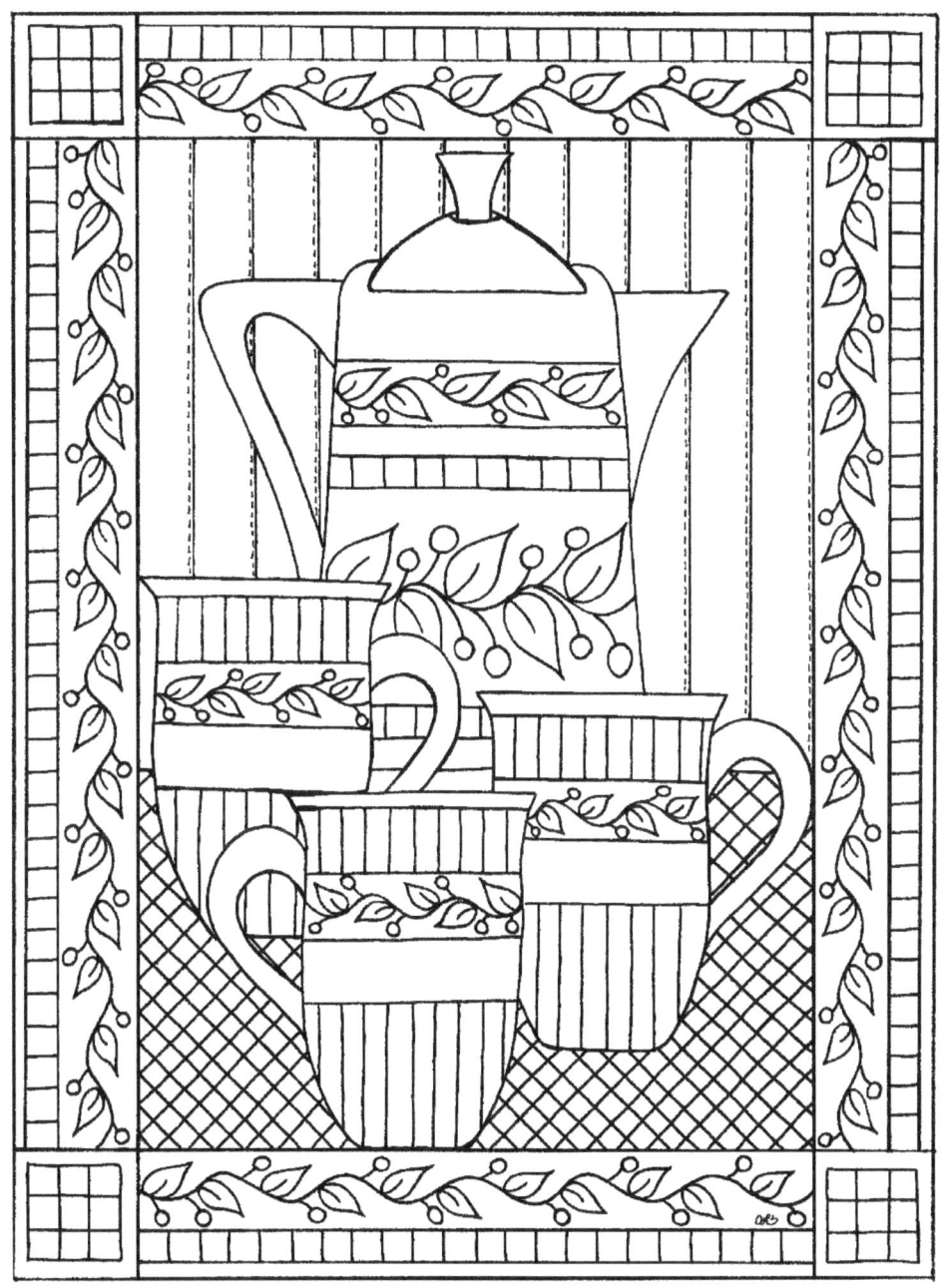

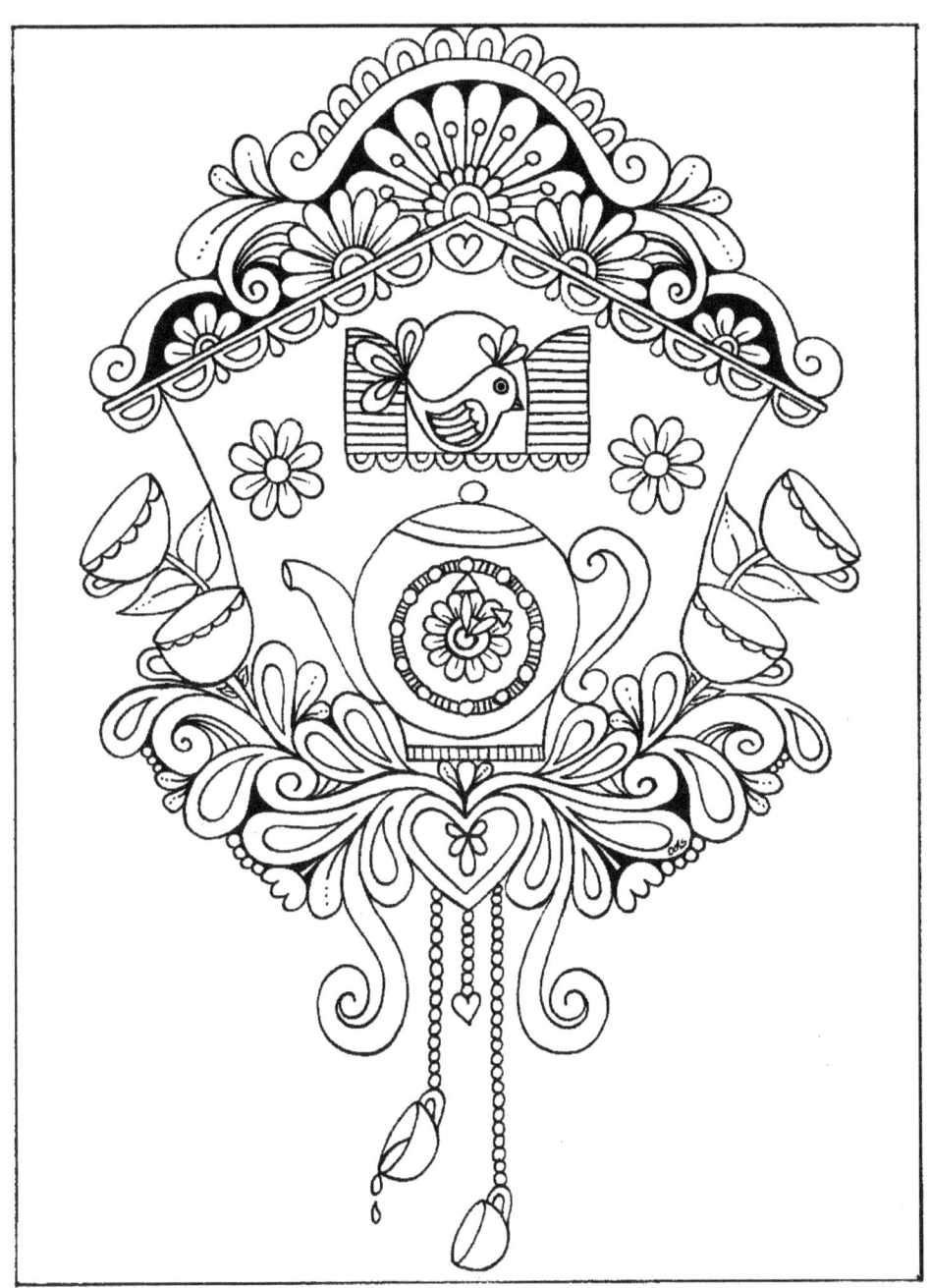

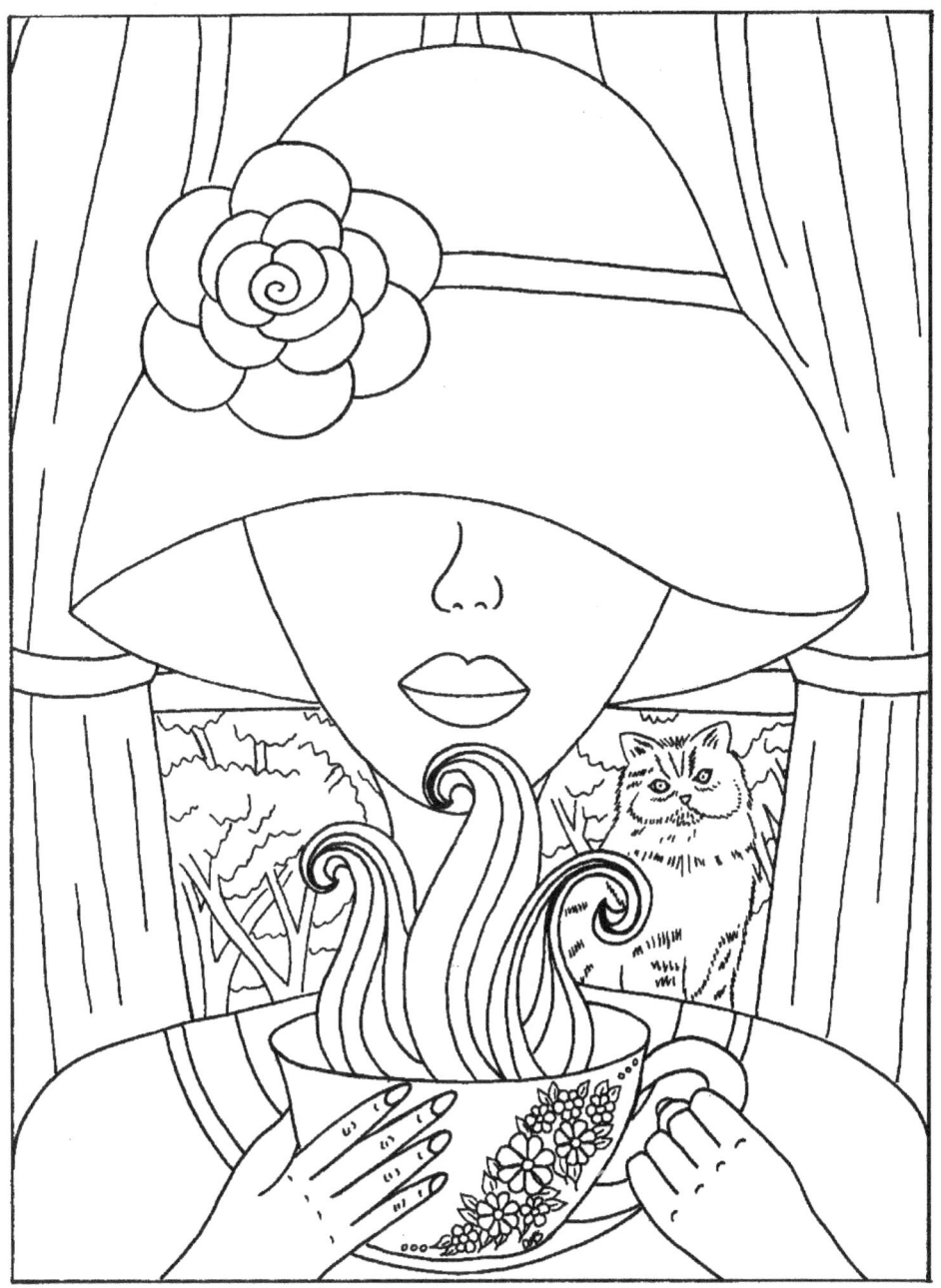

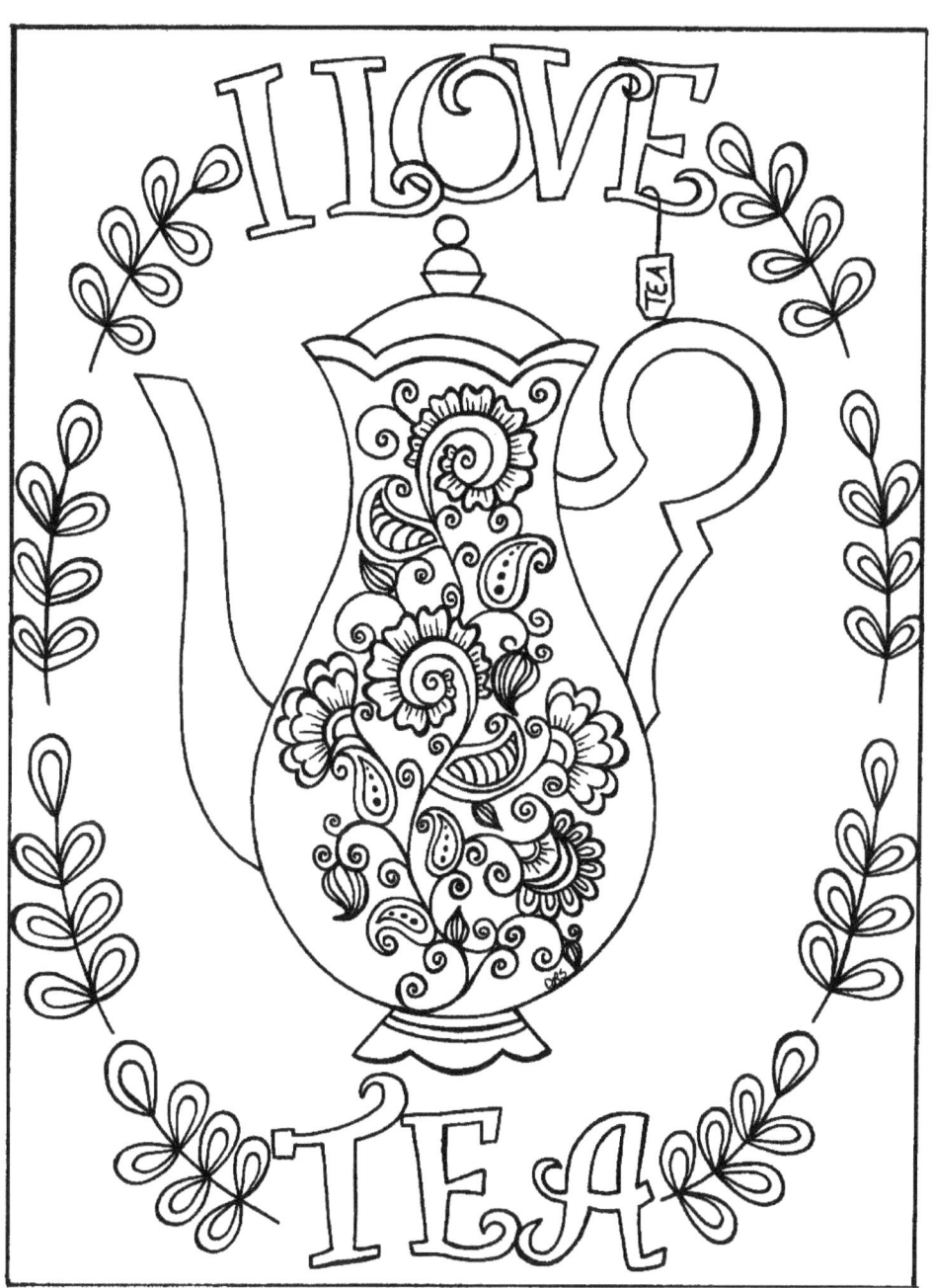

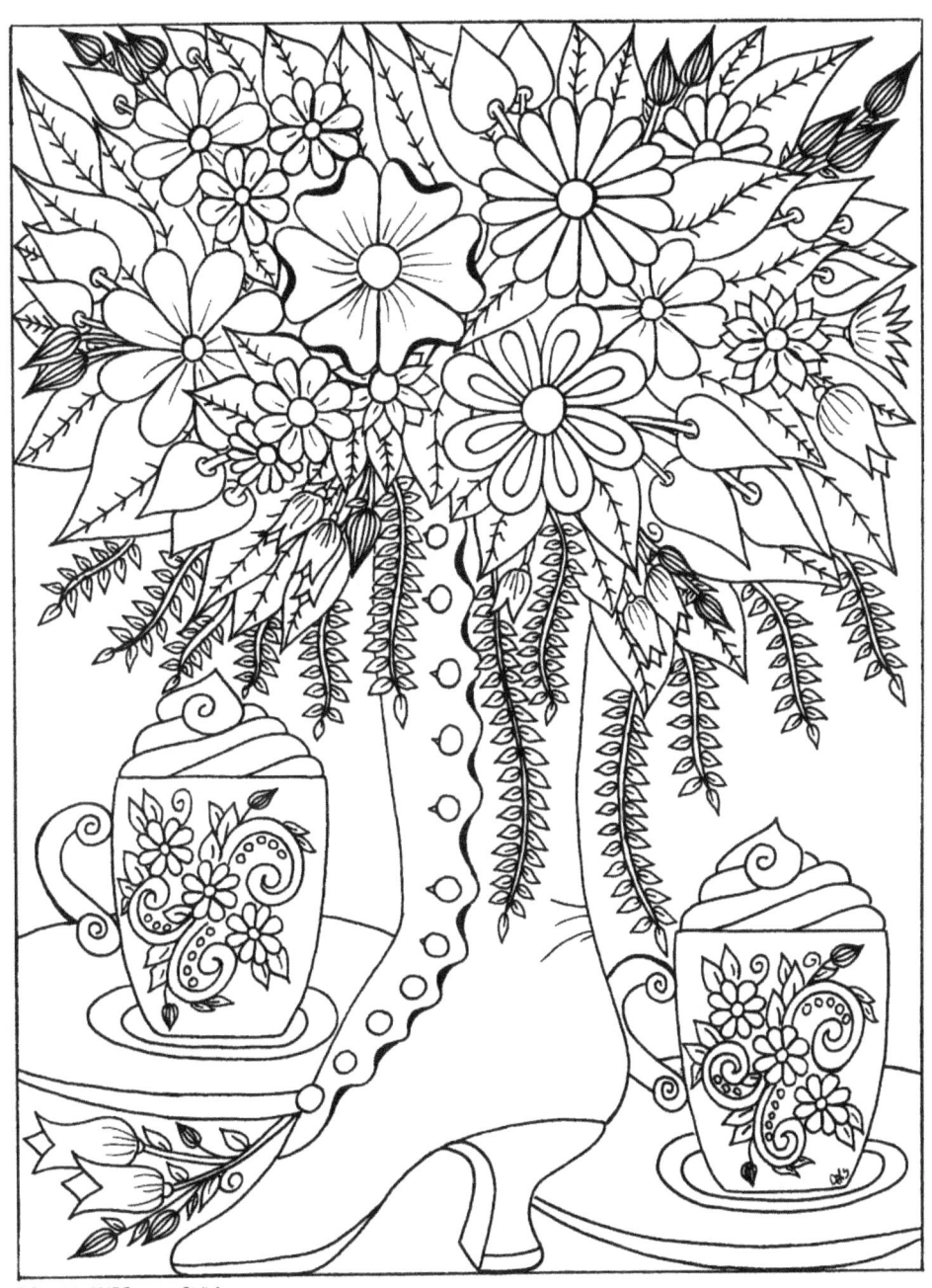

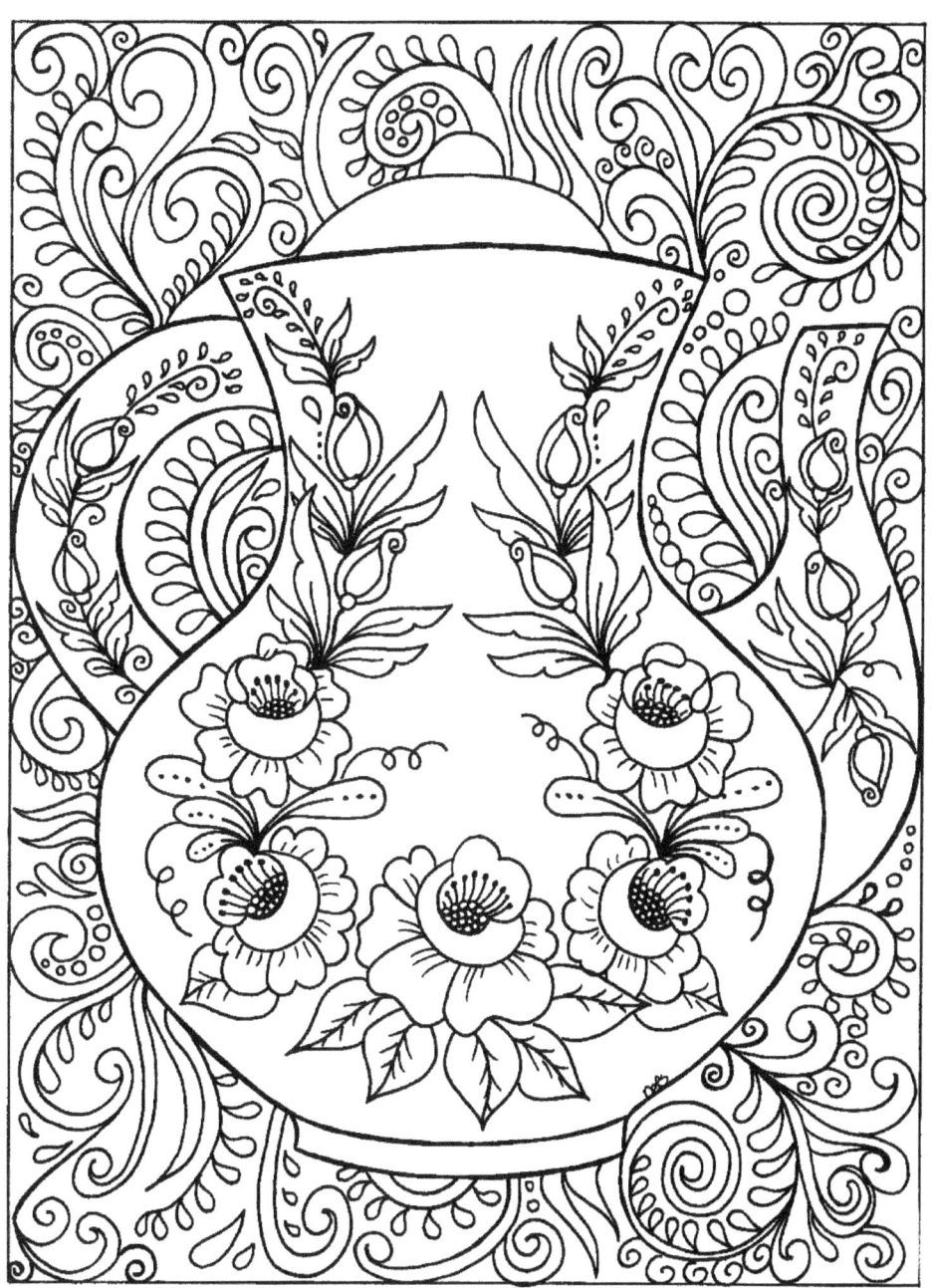

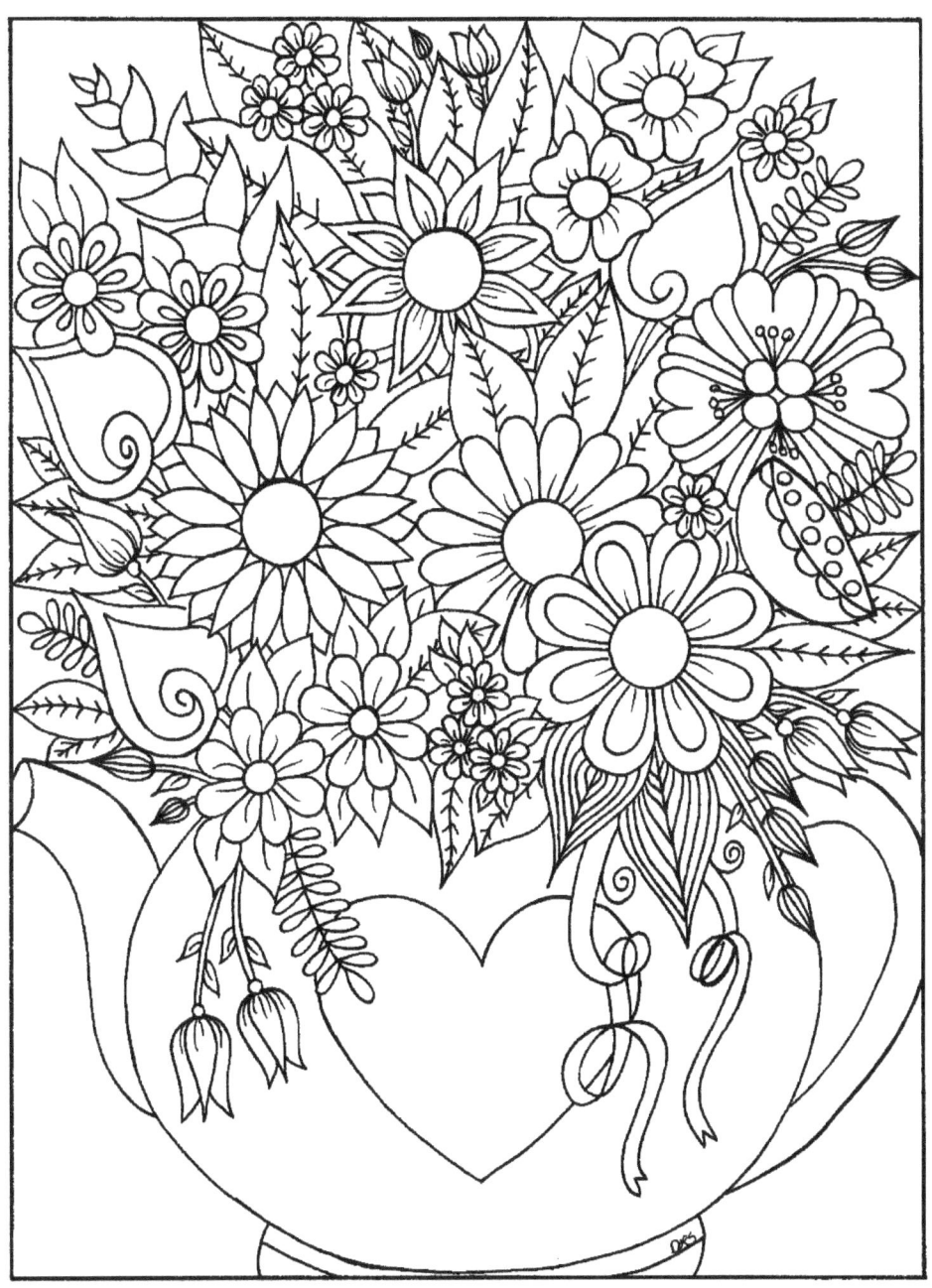

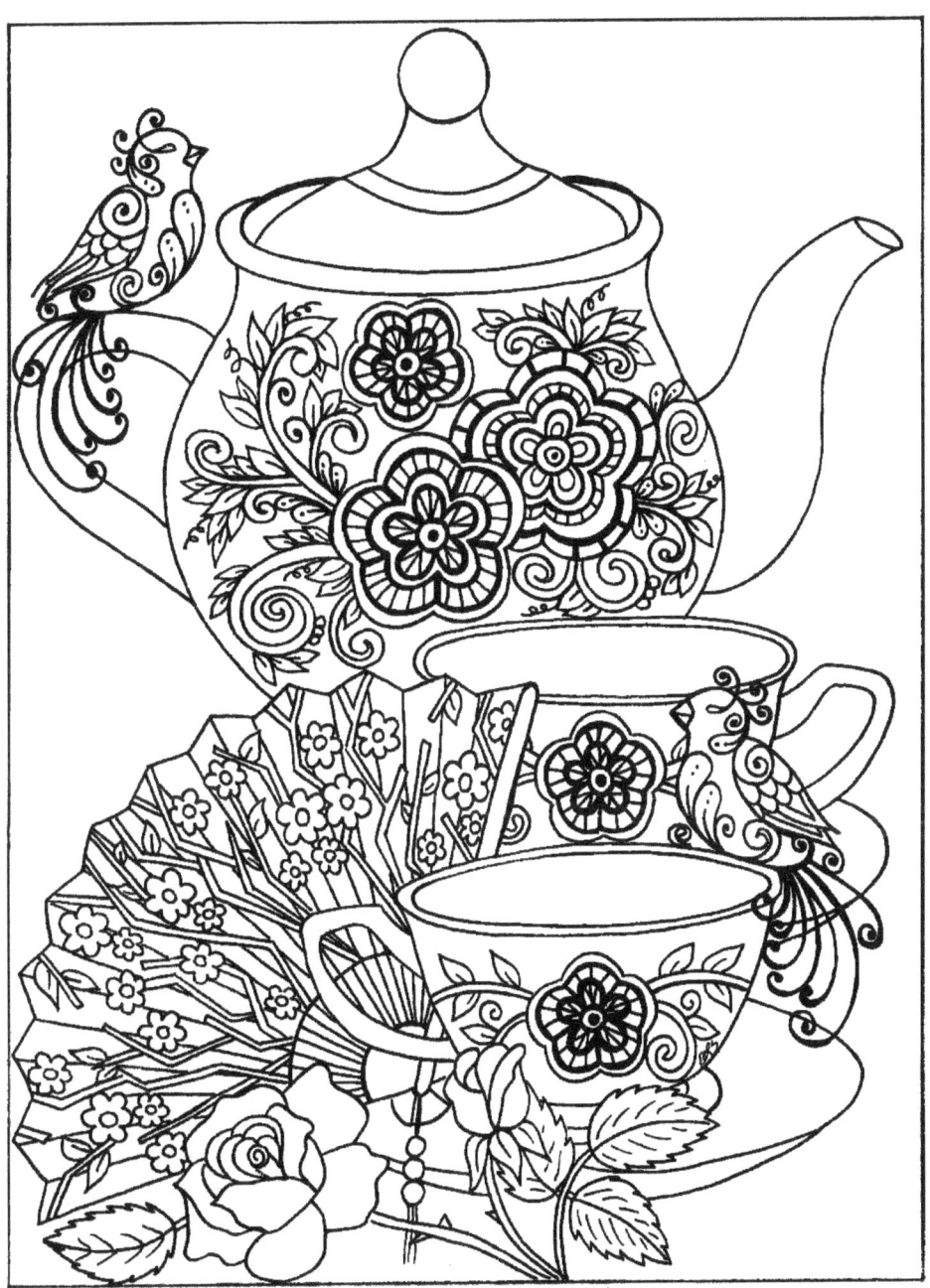

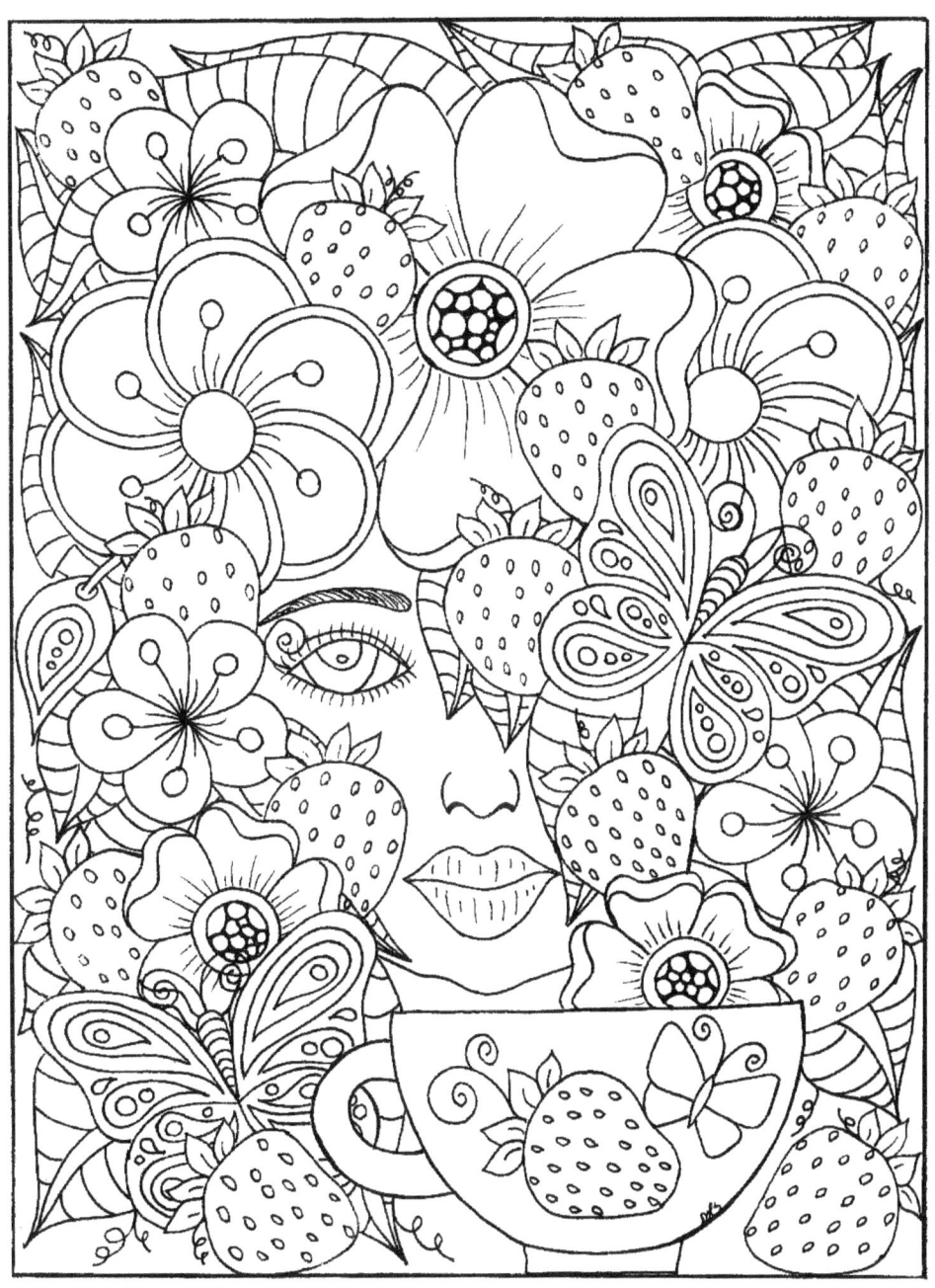

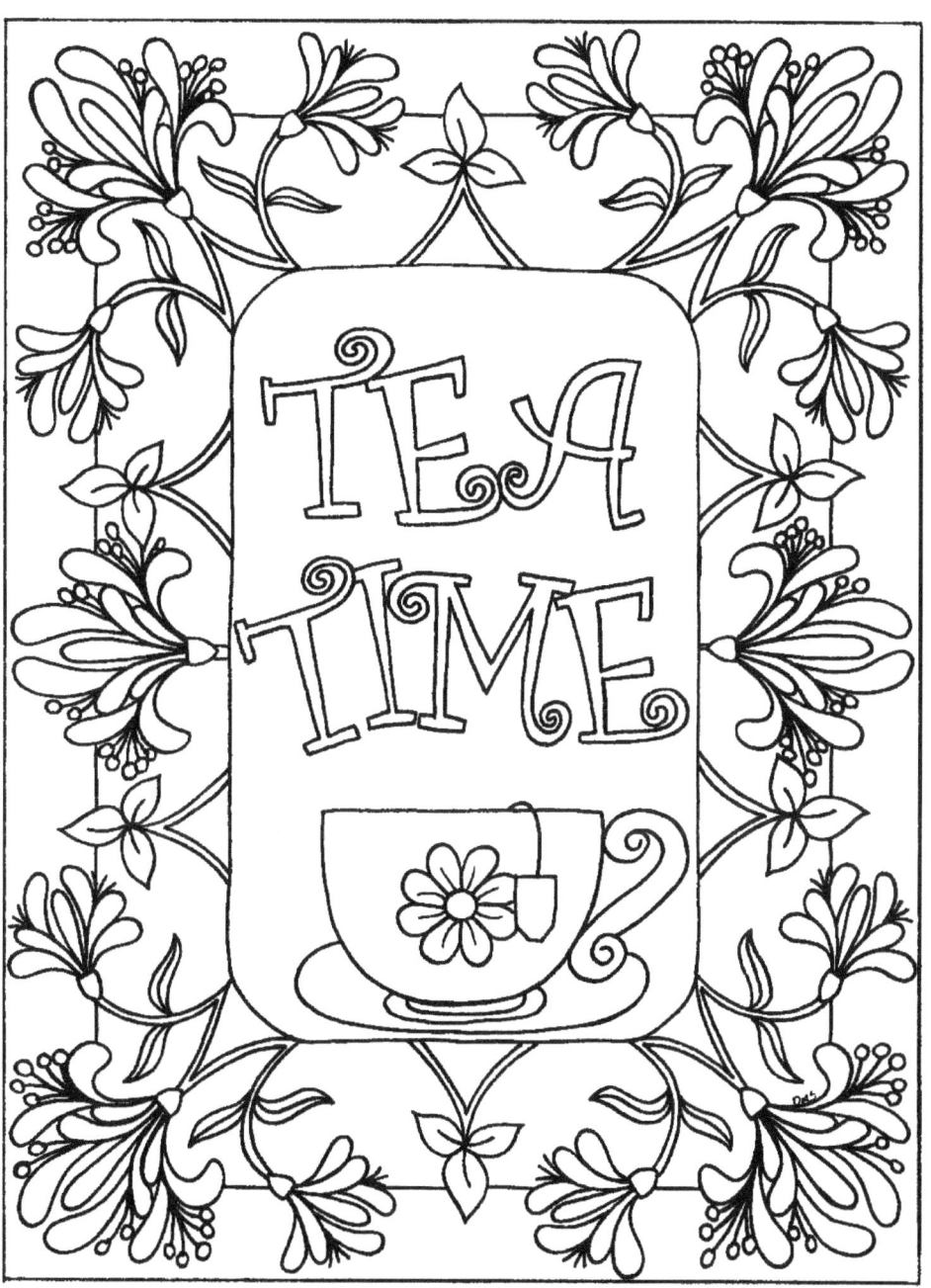

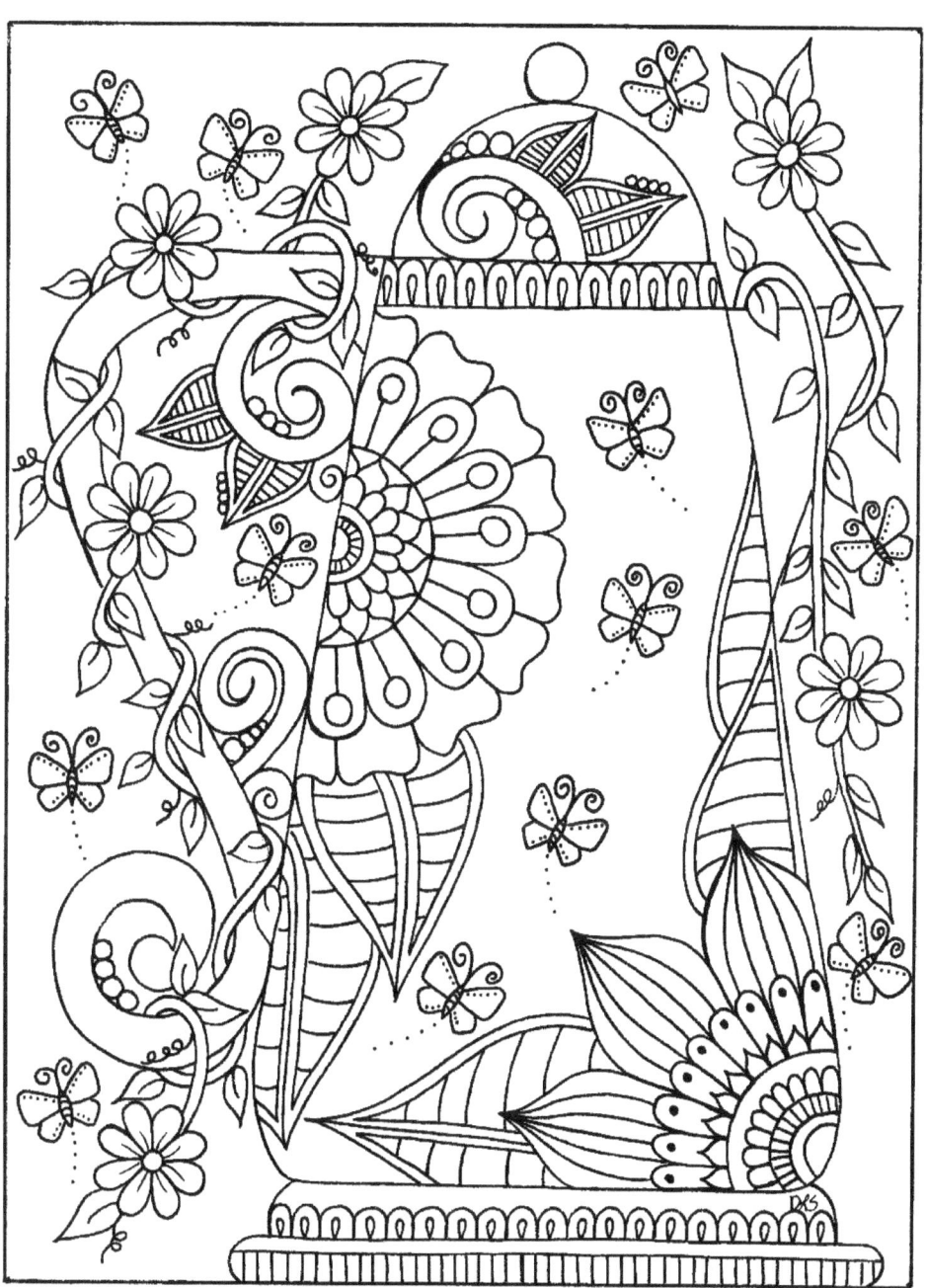

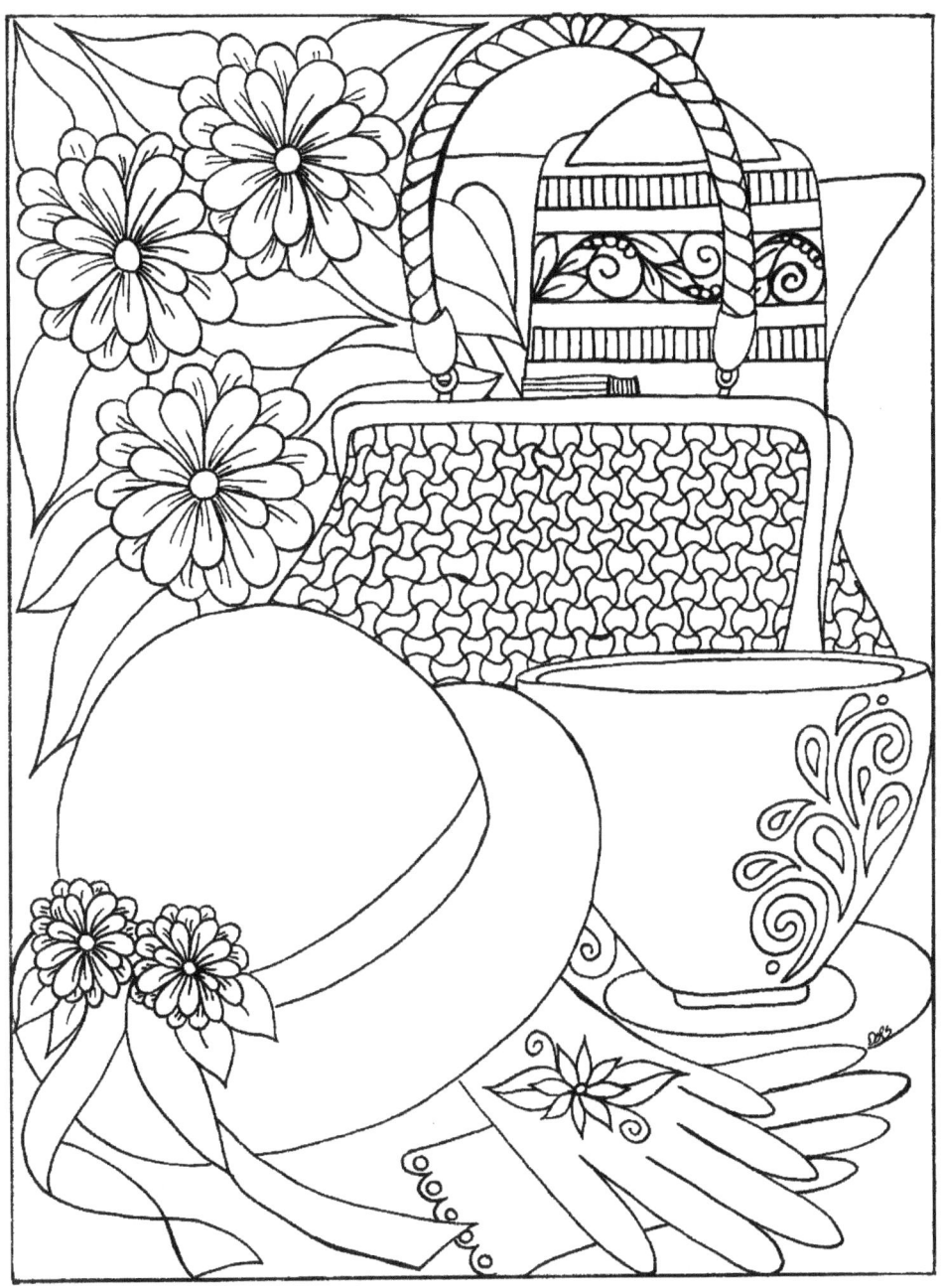

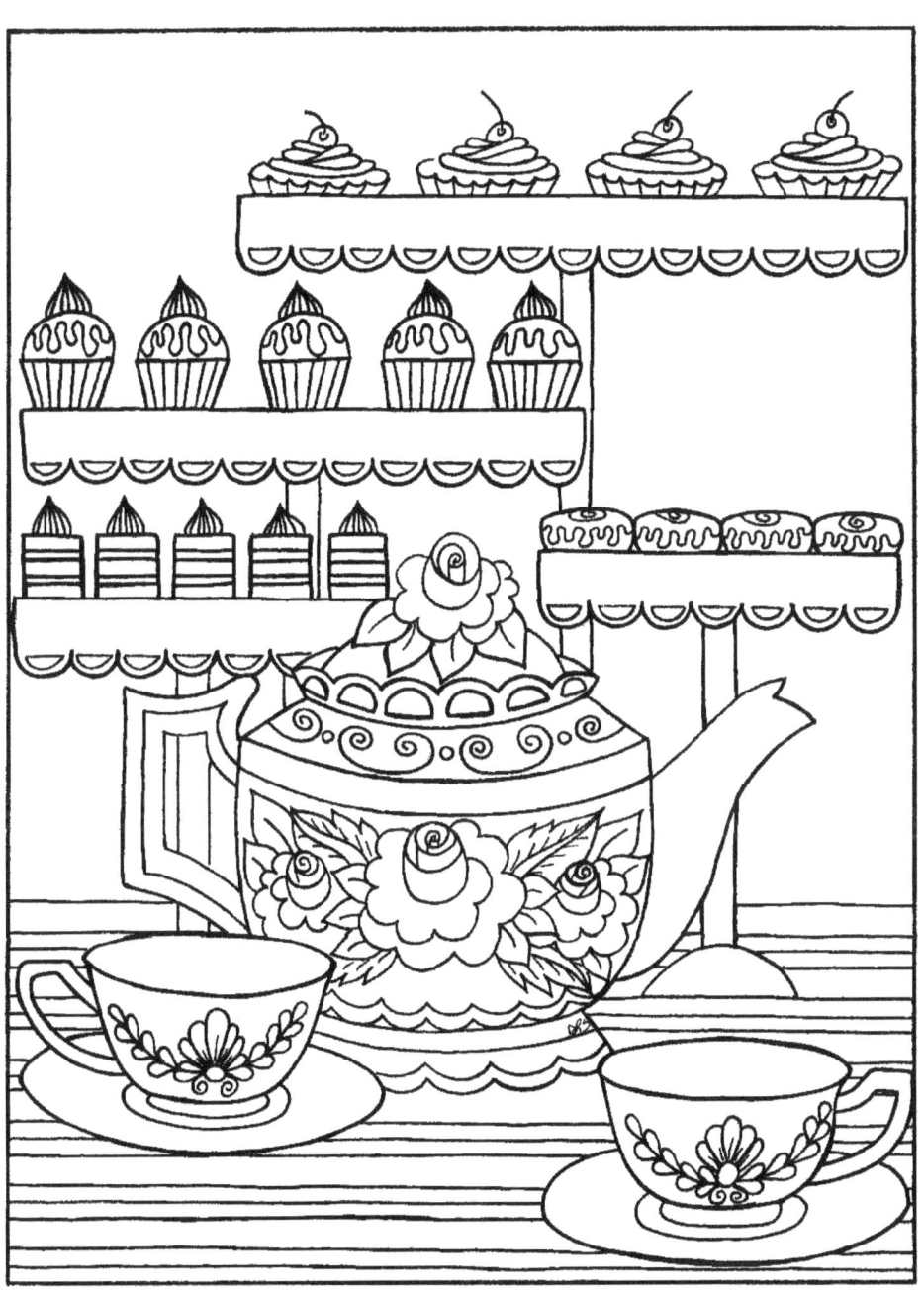

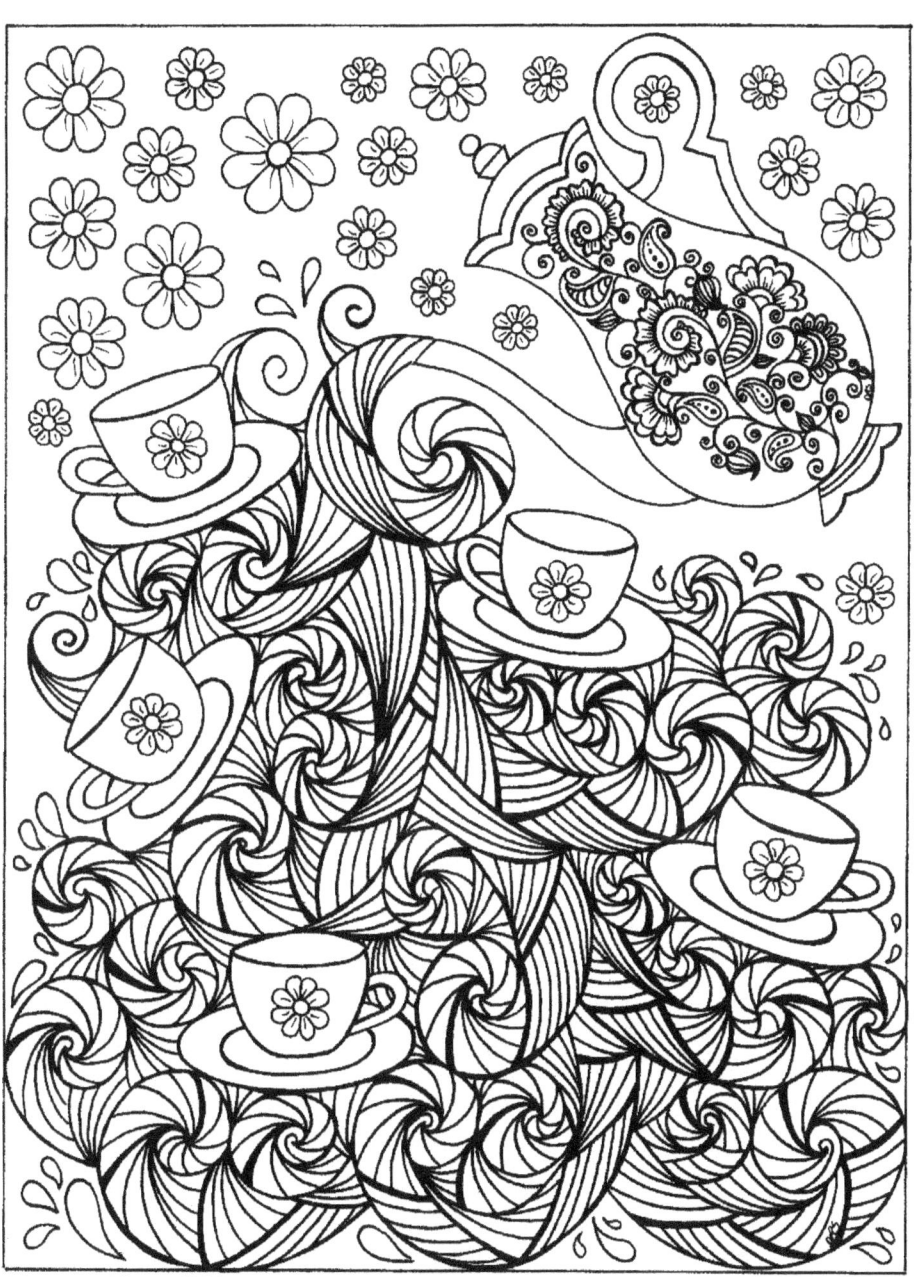

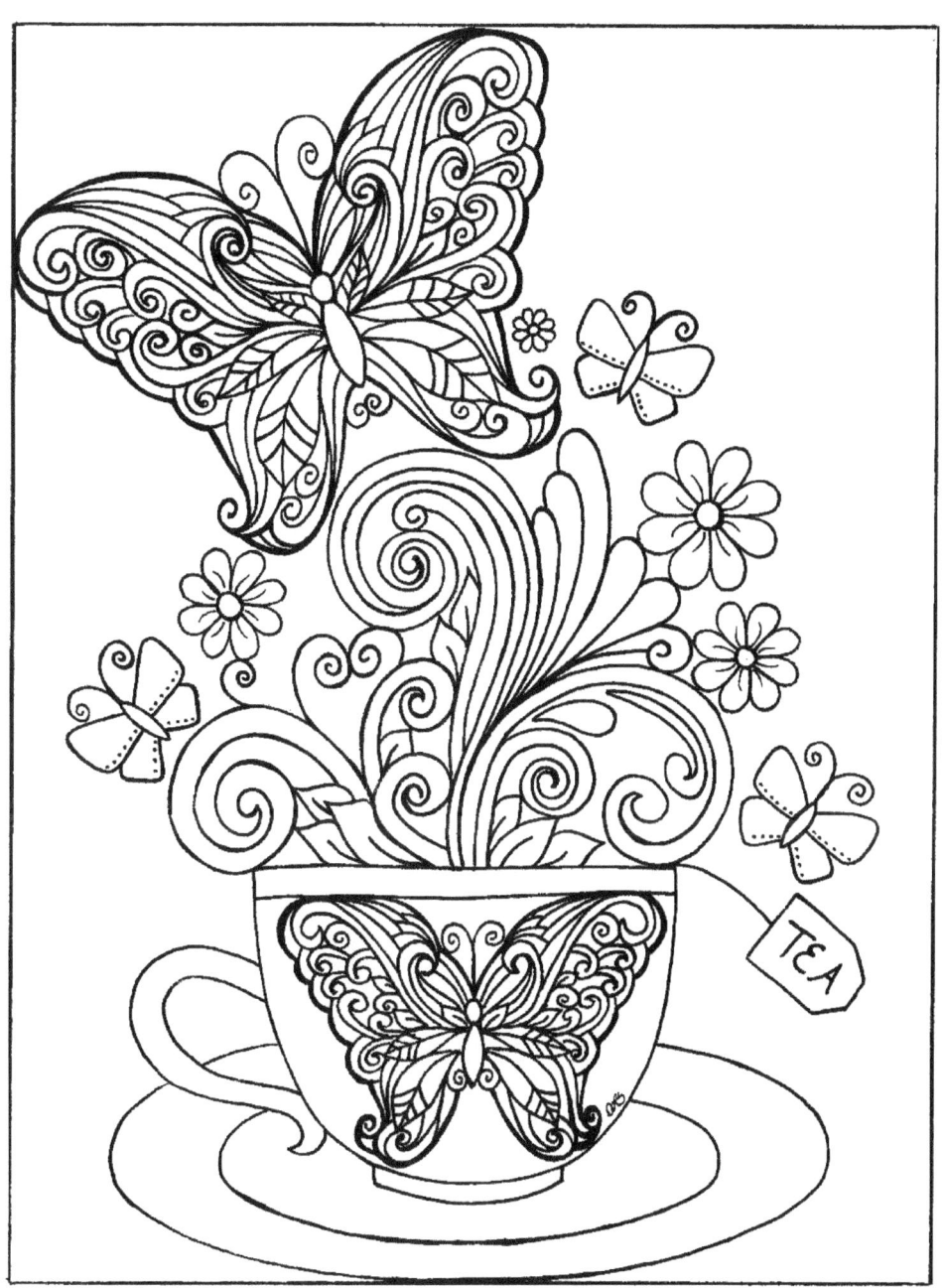

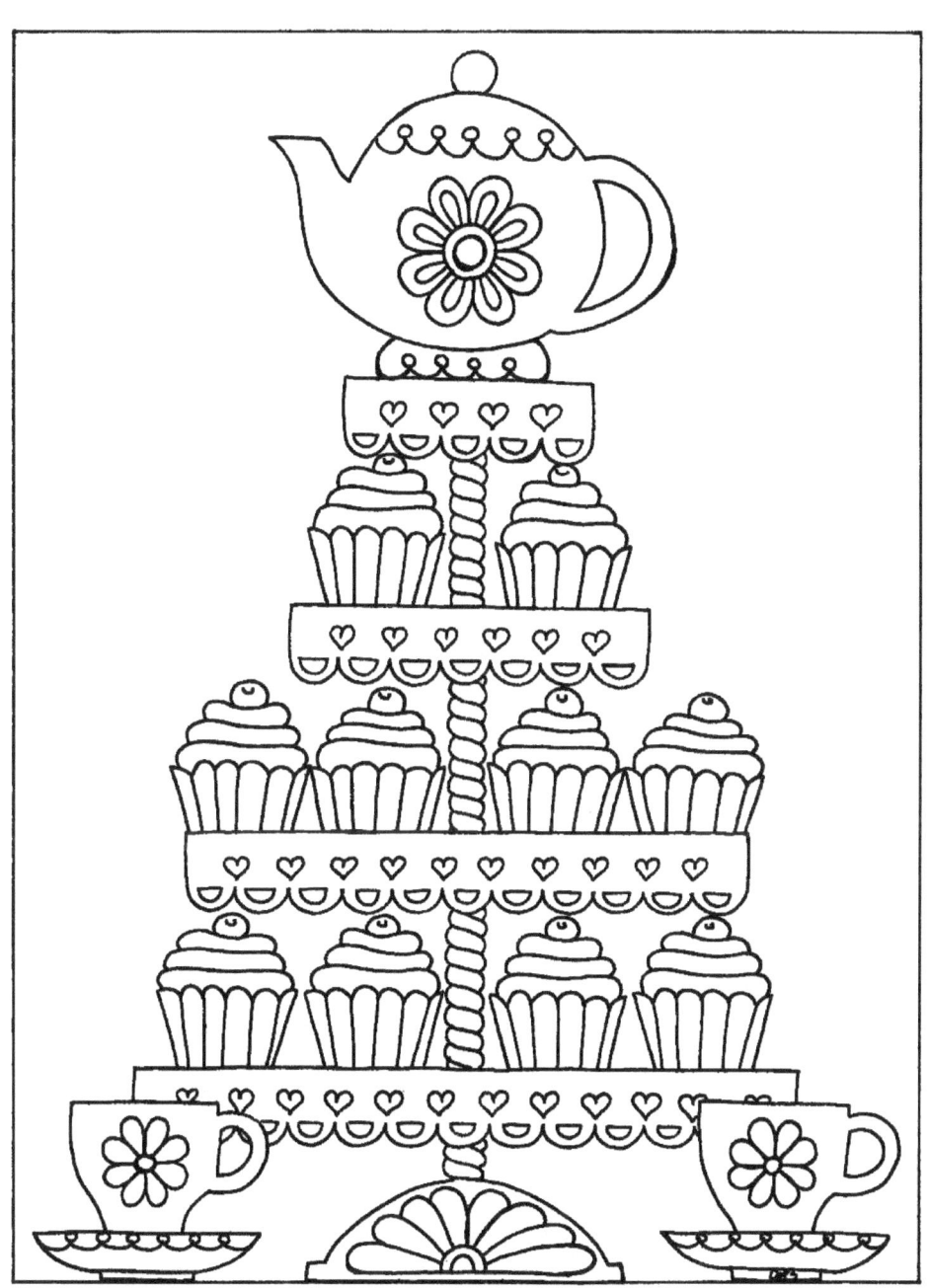

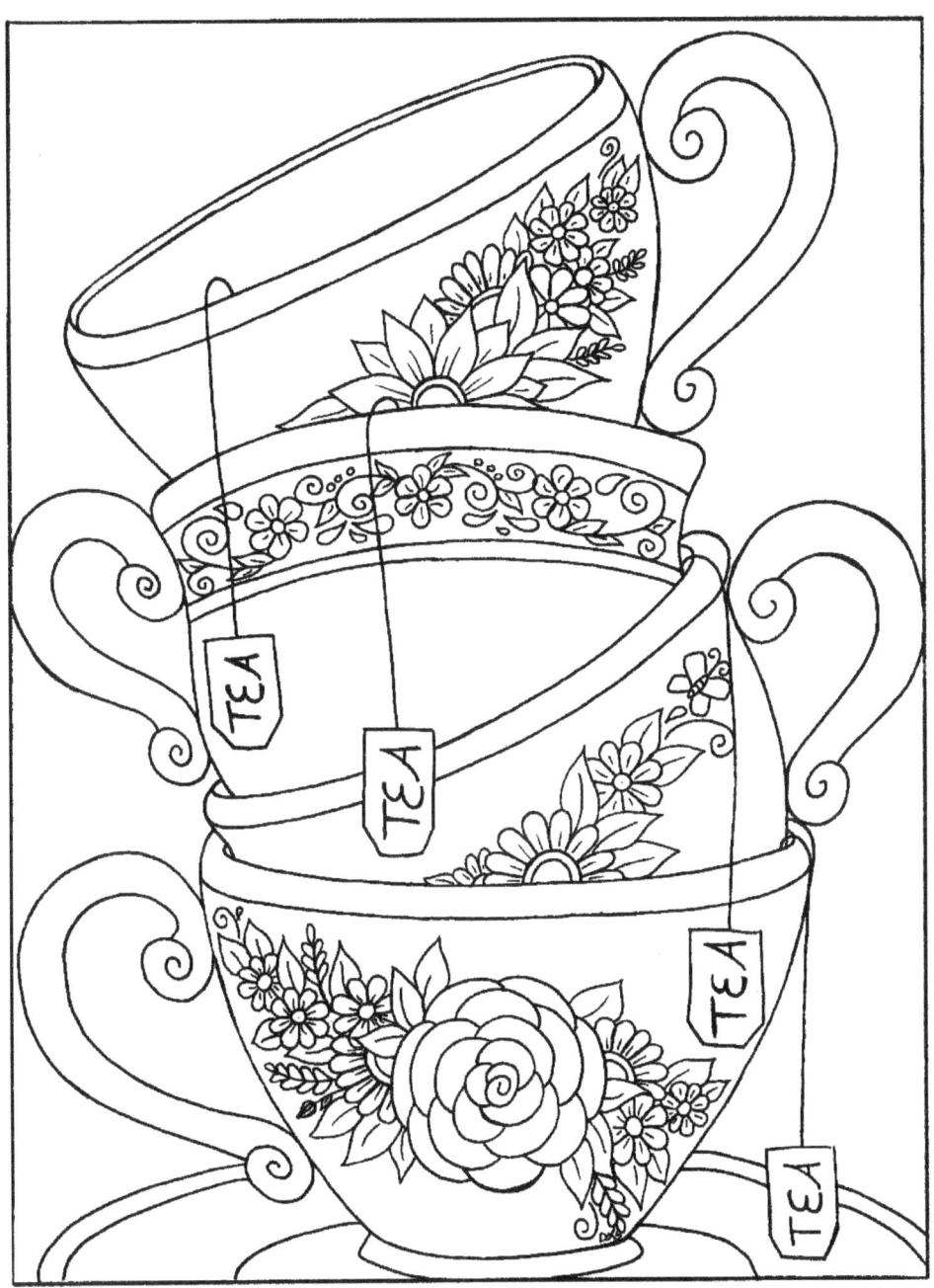

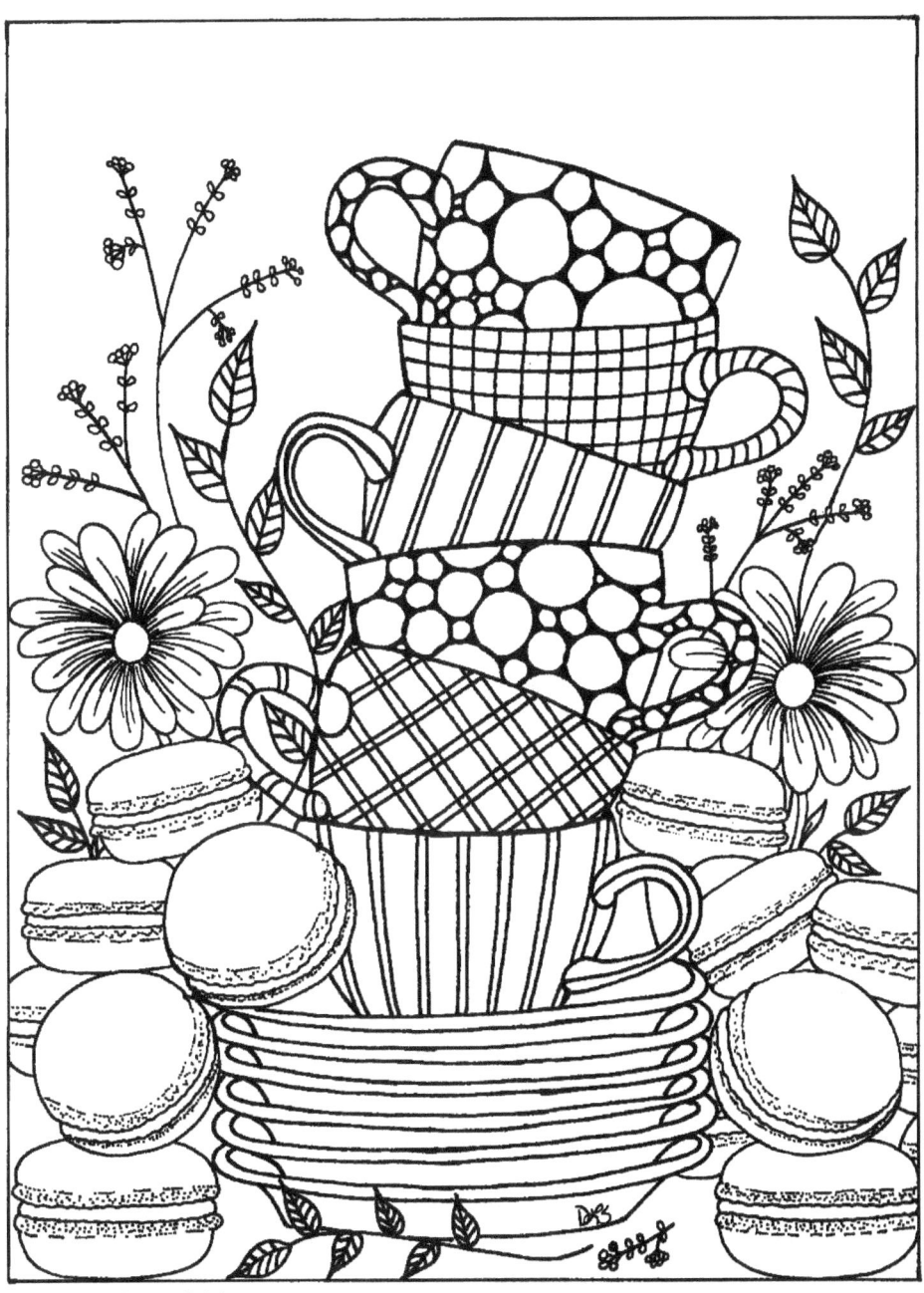

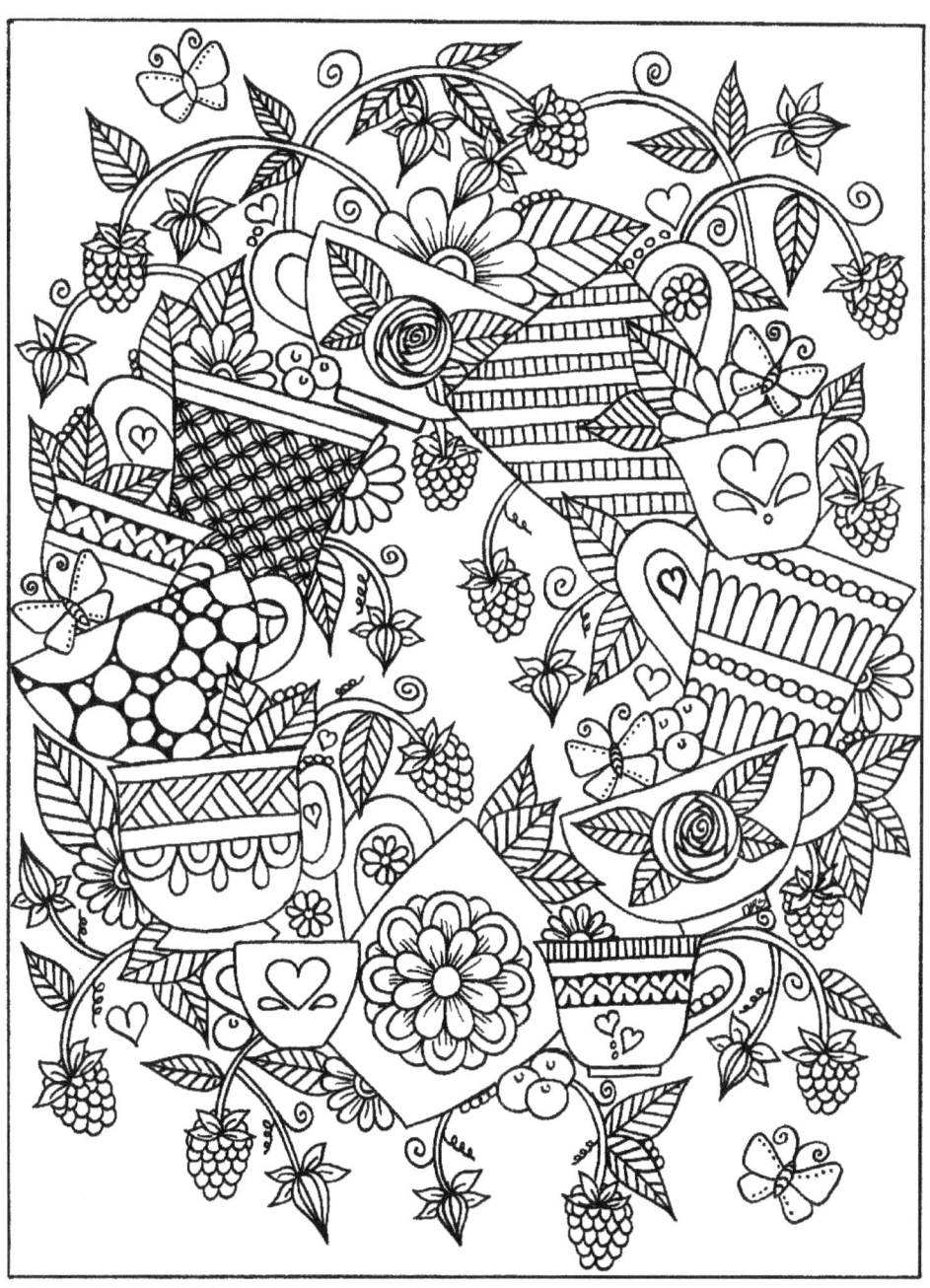

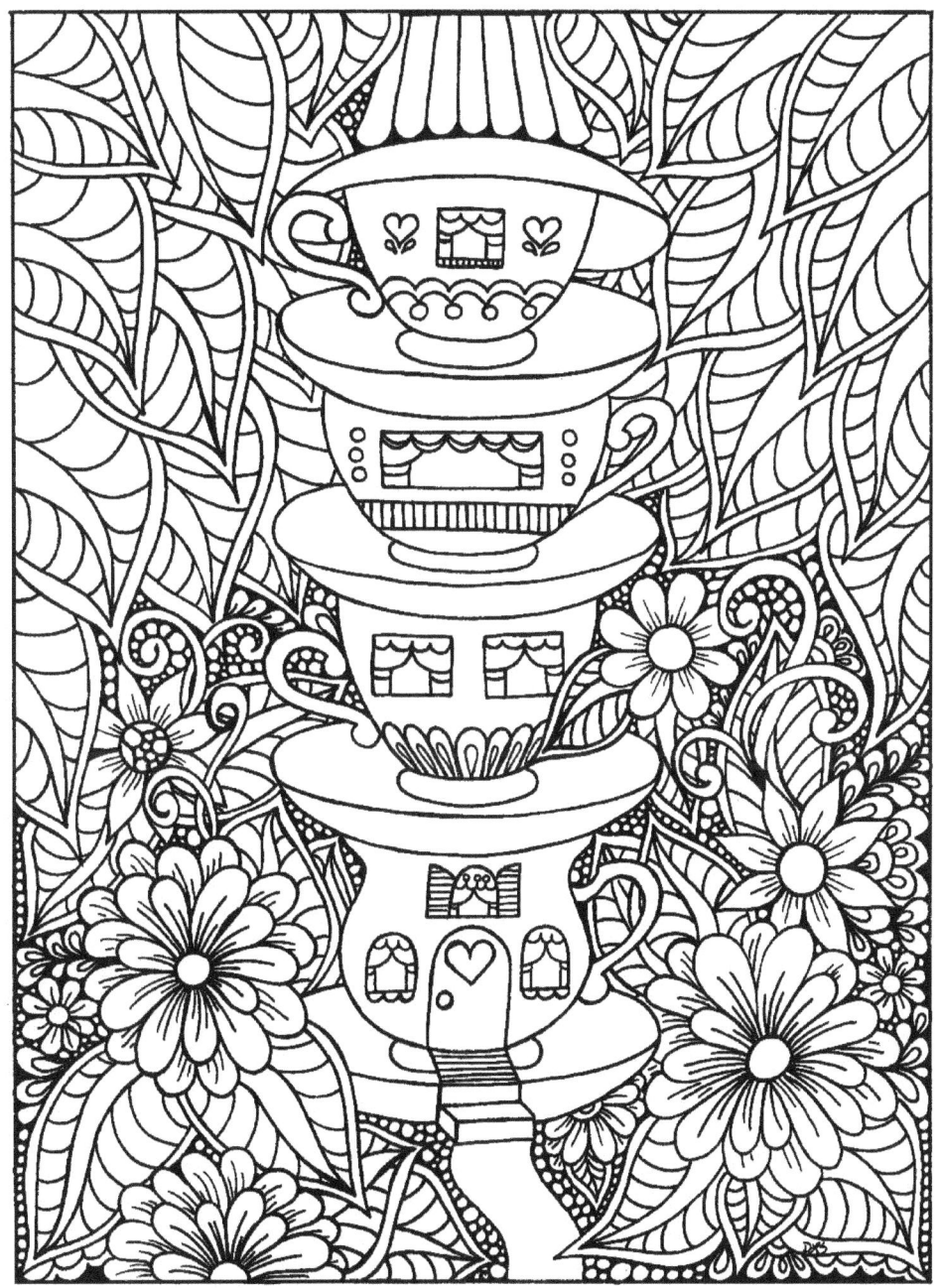
© Copyright 2017 Dwyanna Stoltzfus

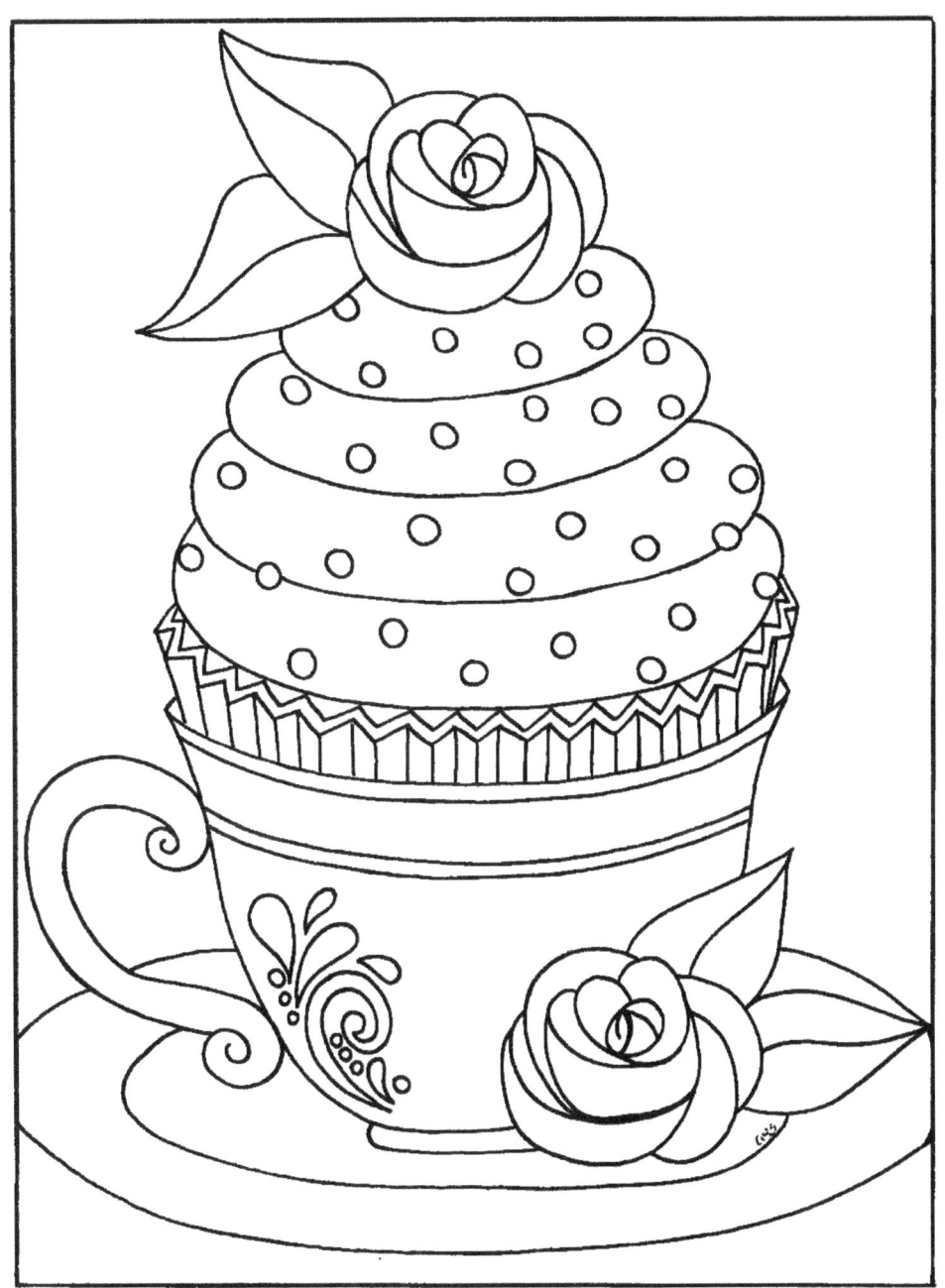

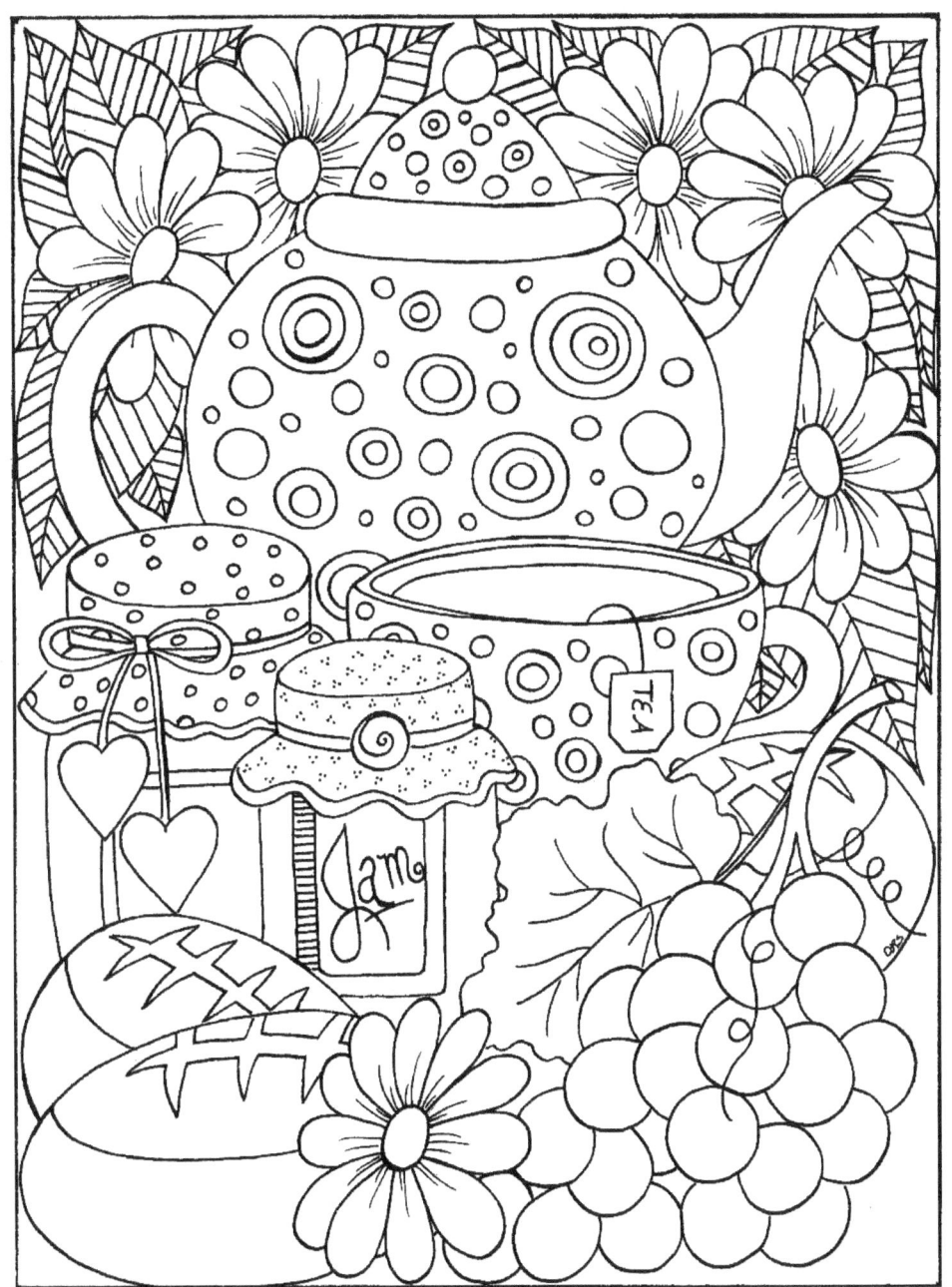

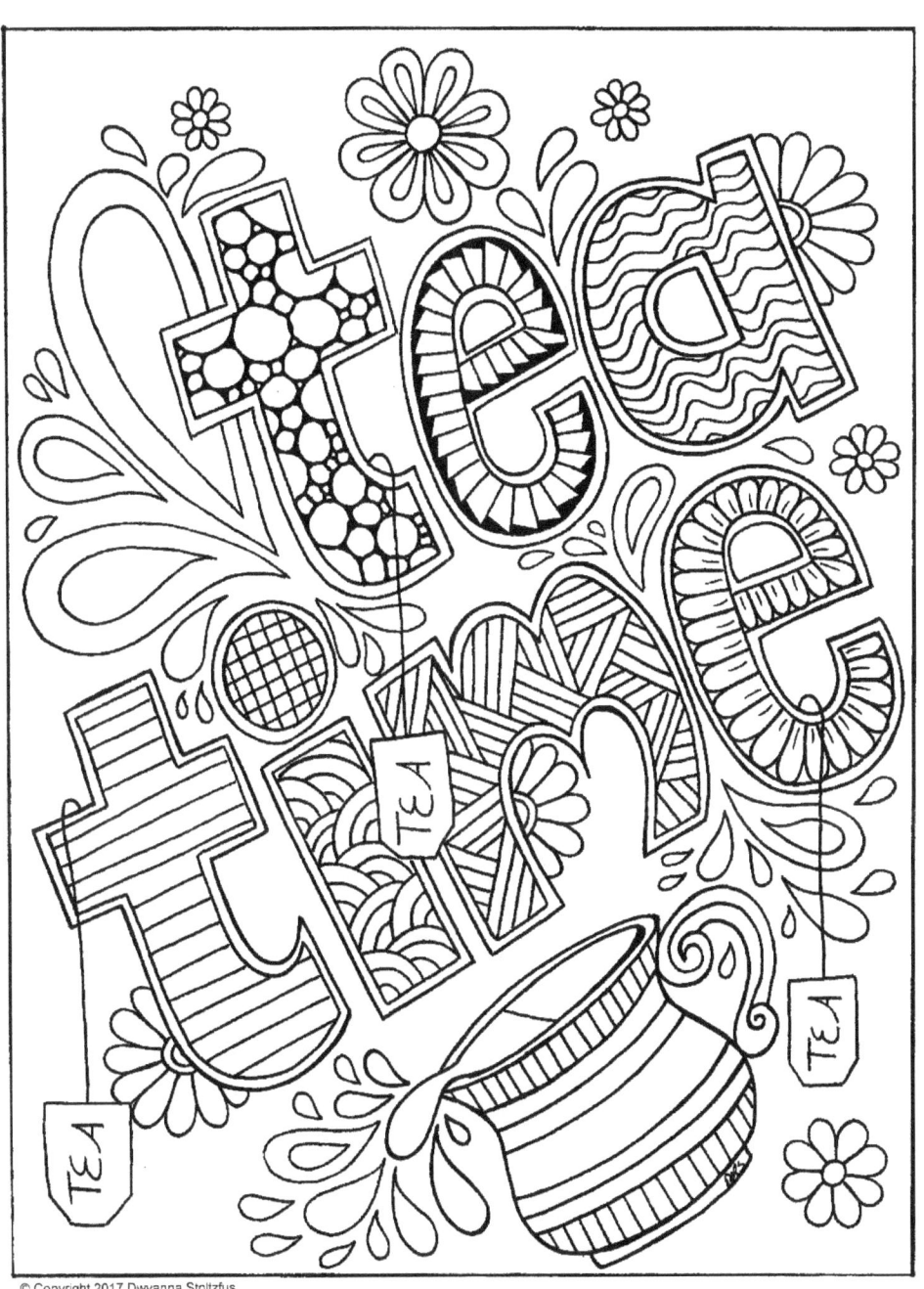

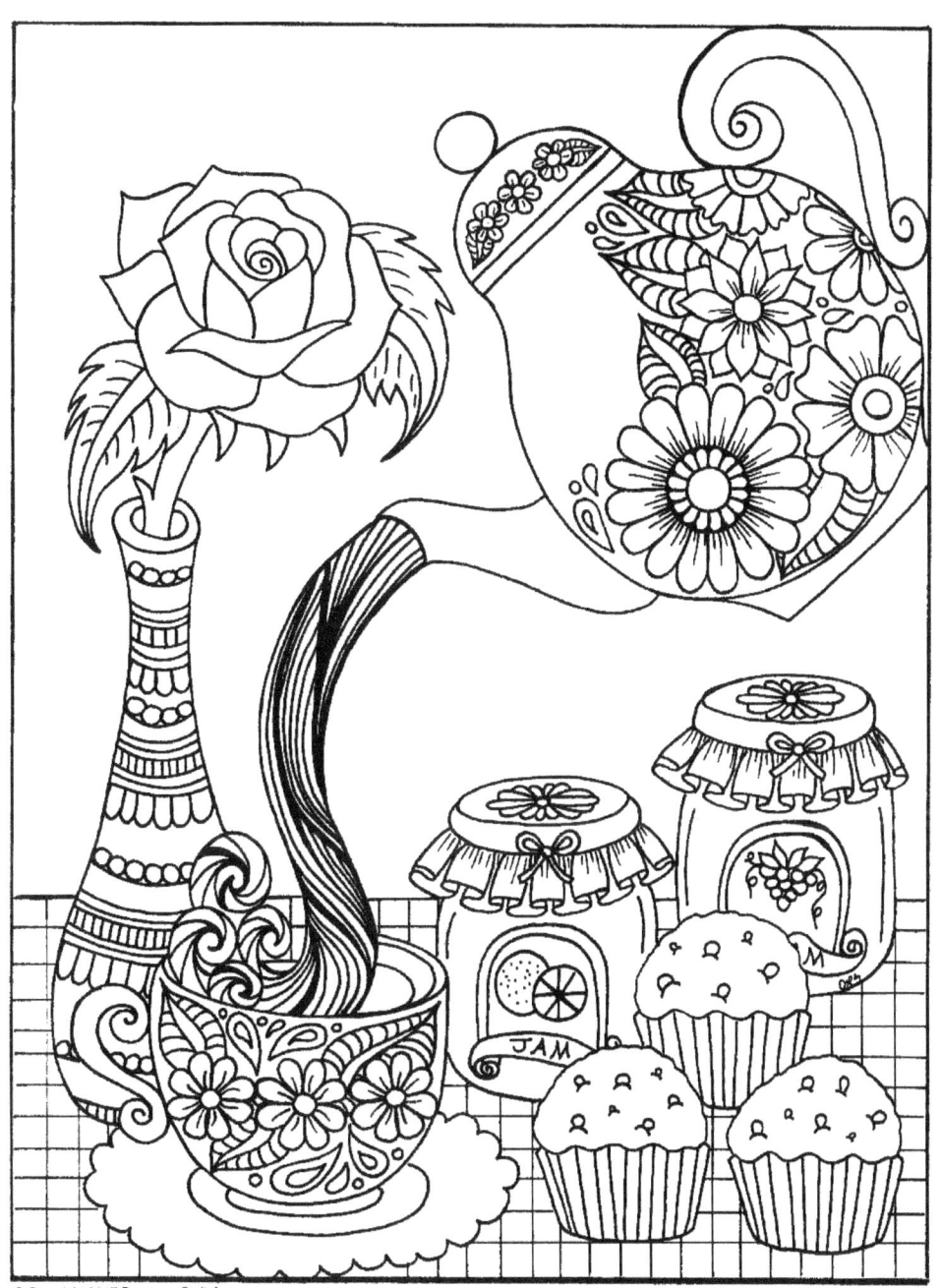

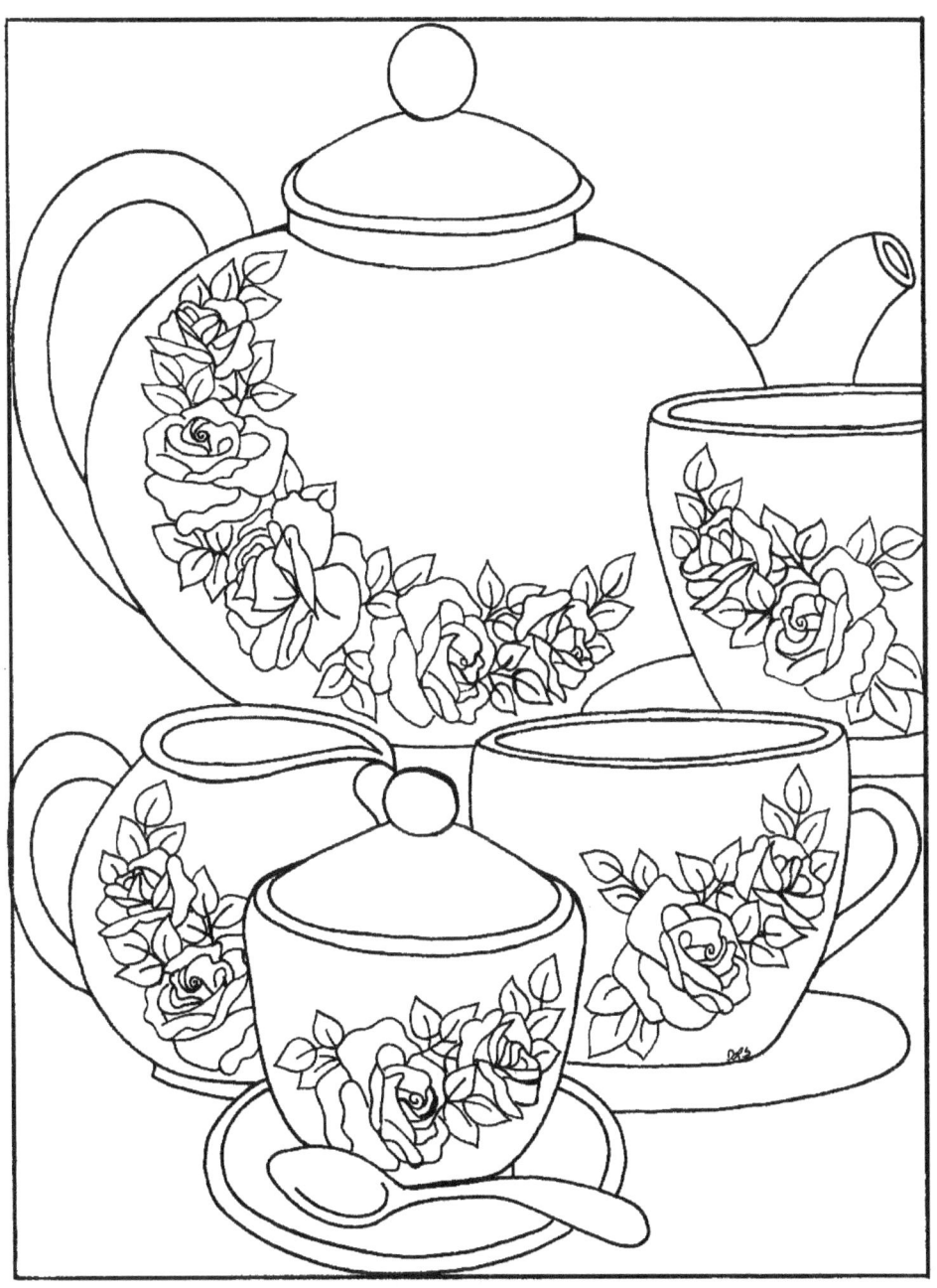

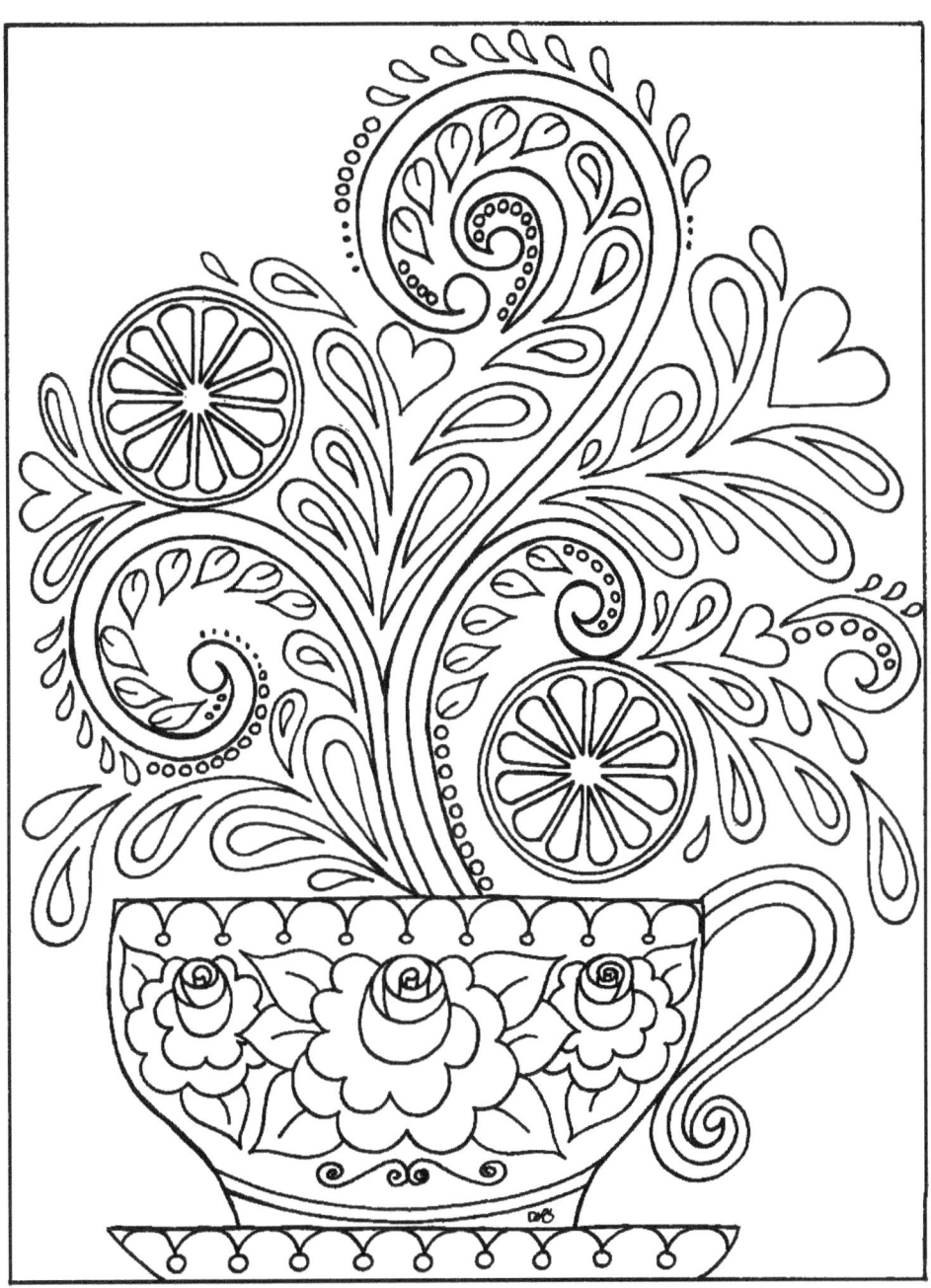

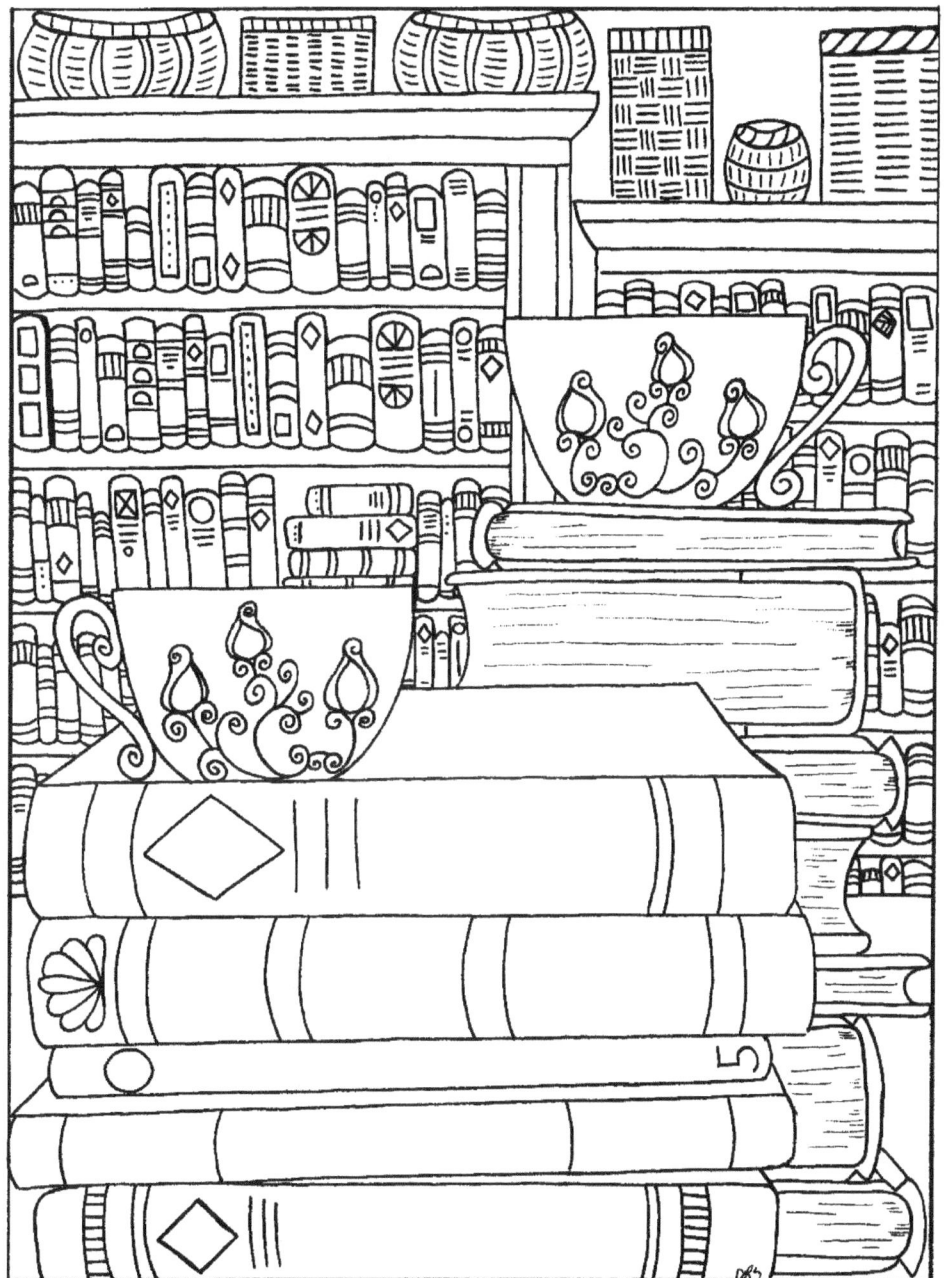

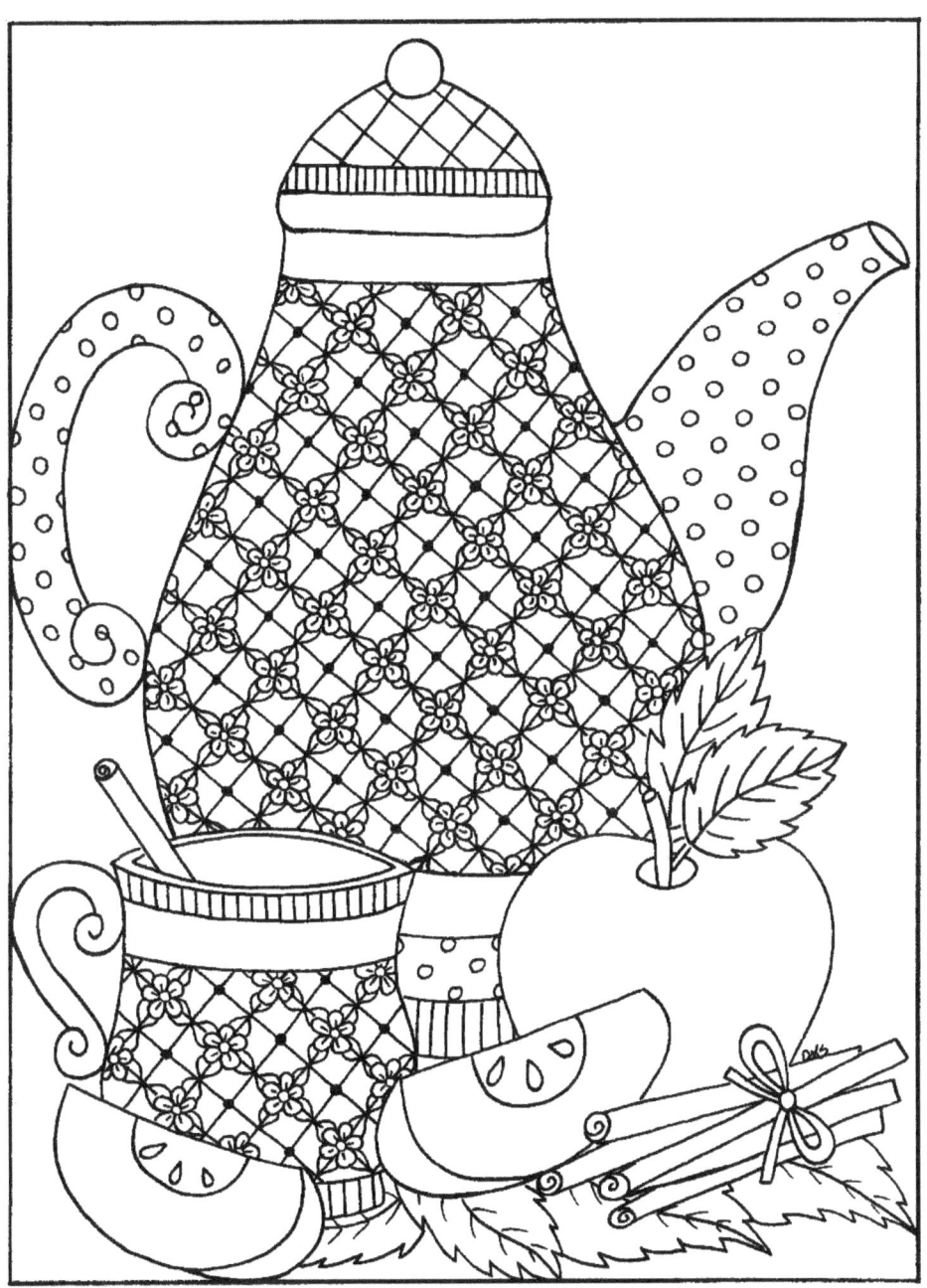

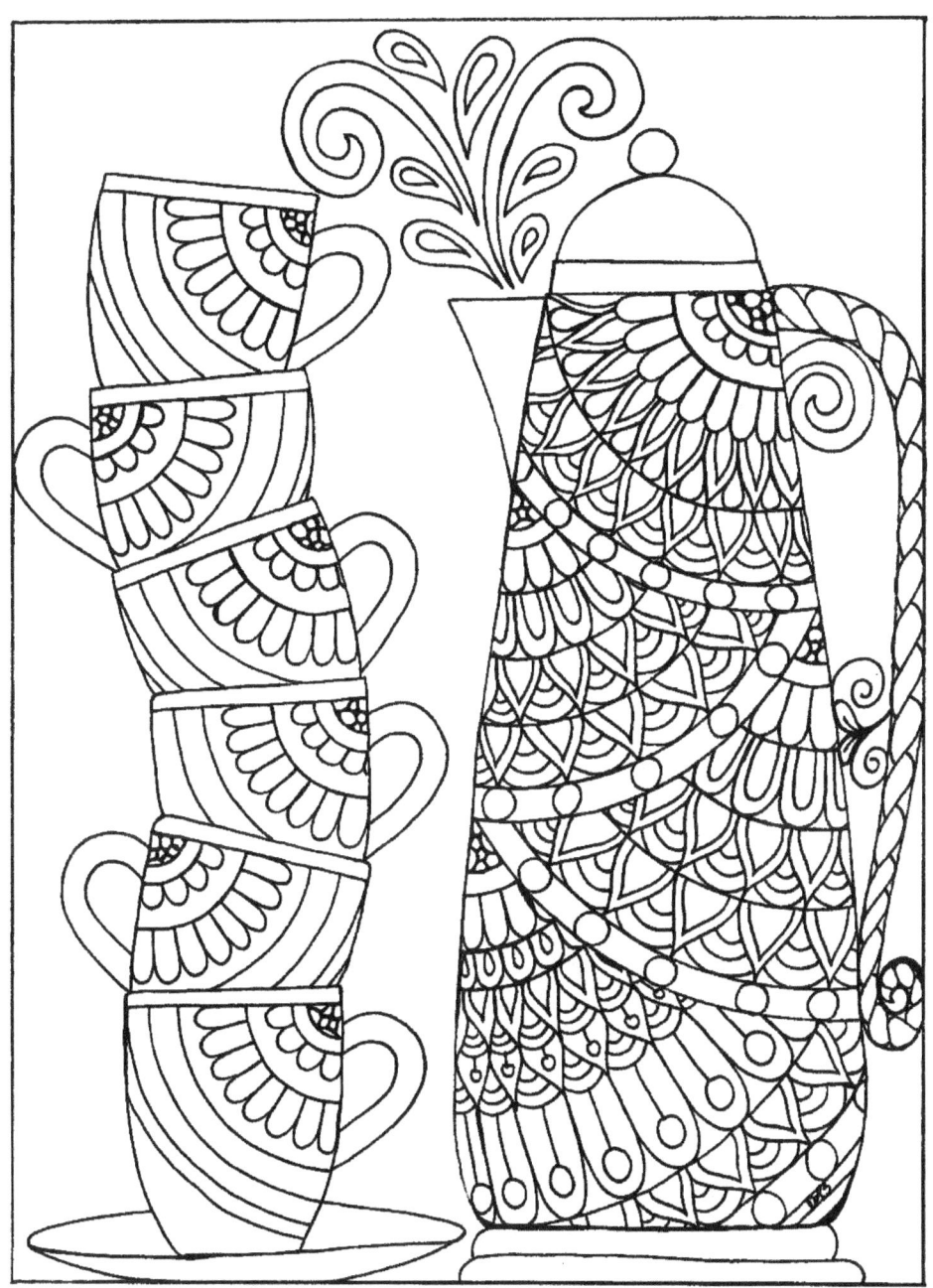

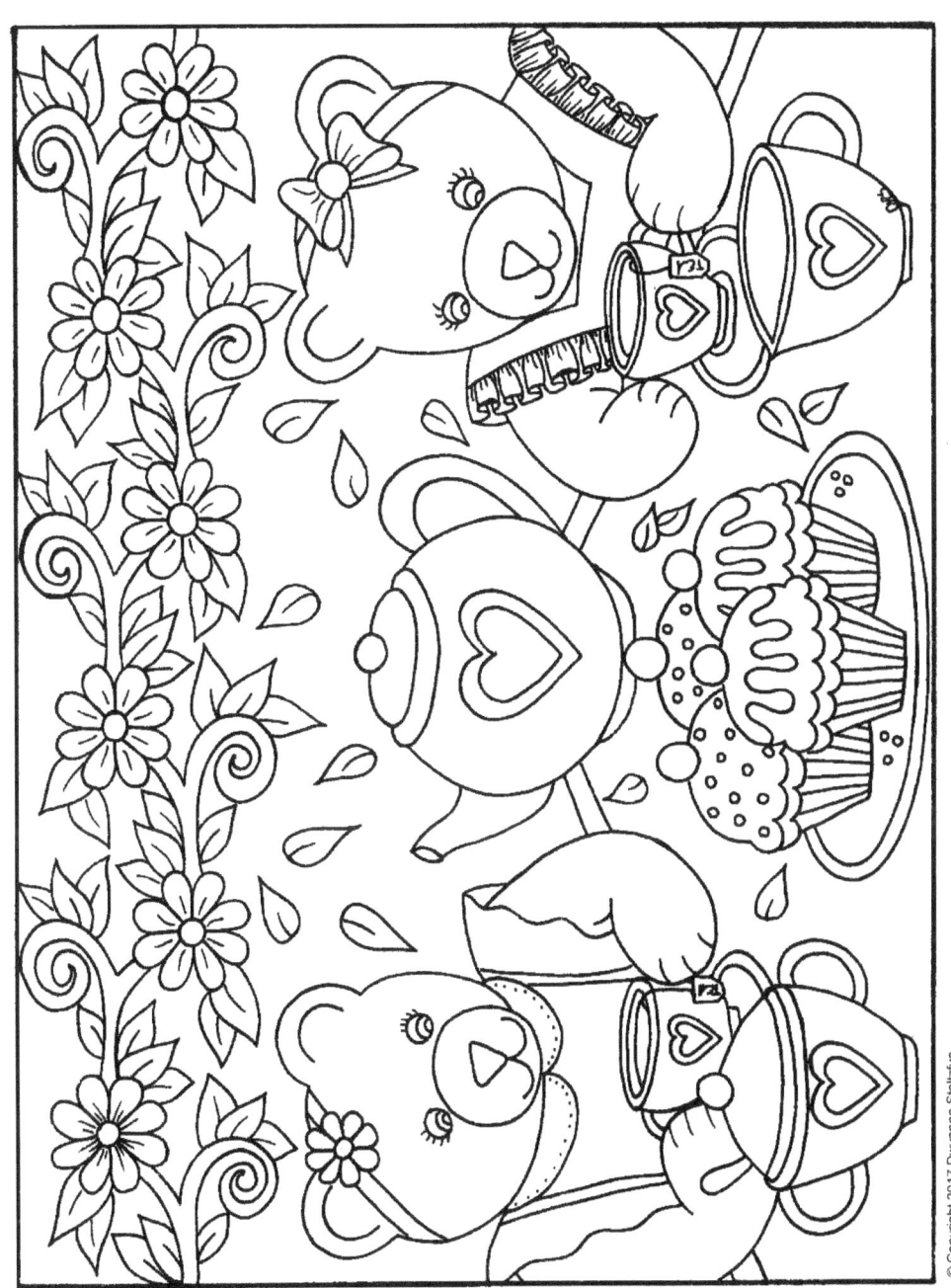

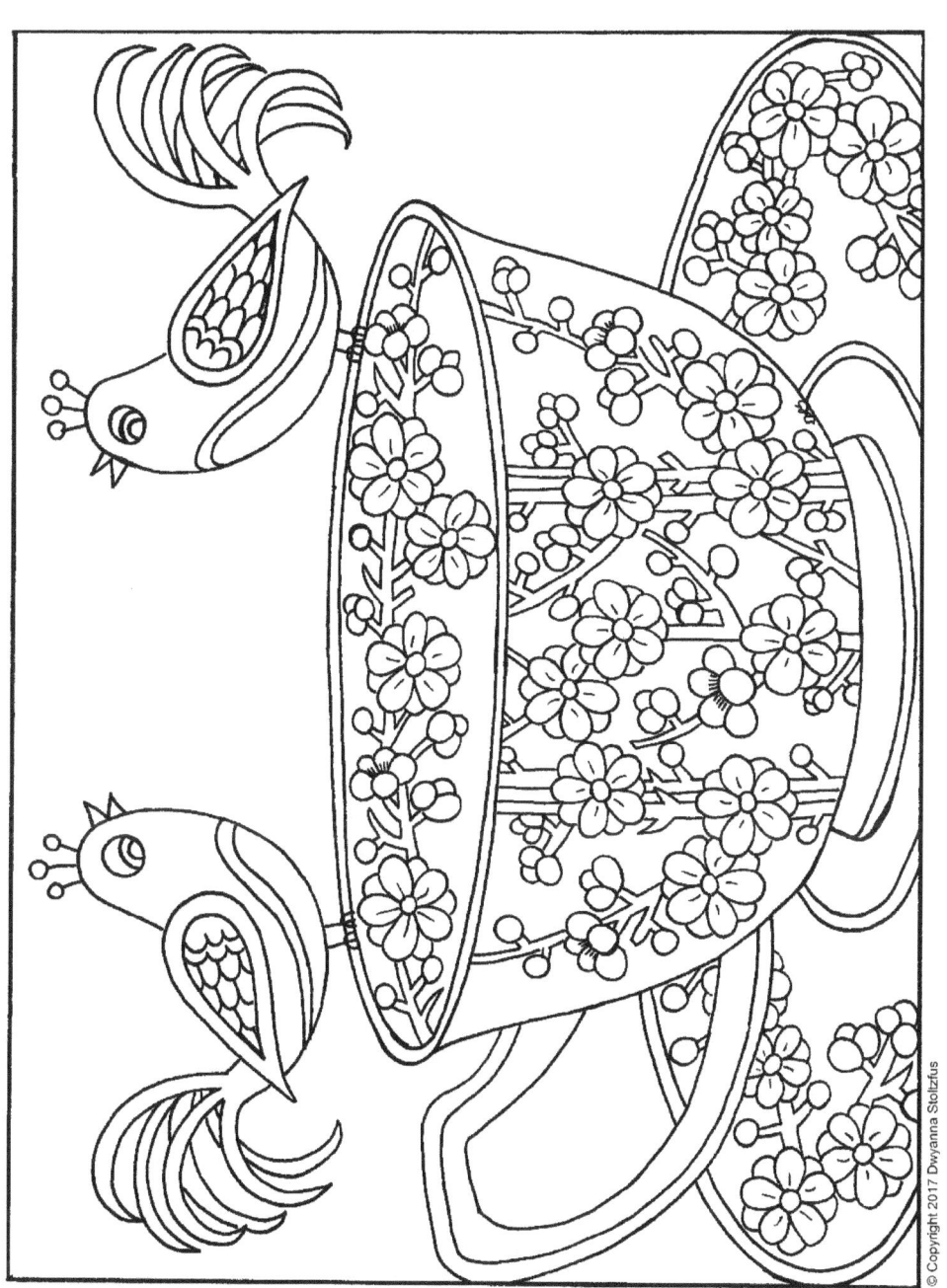

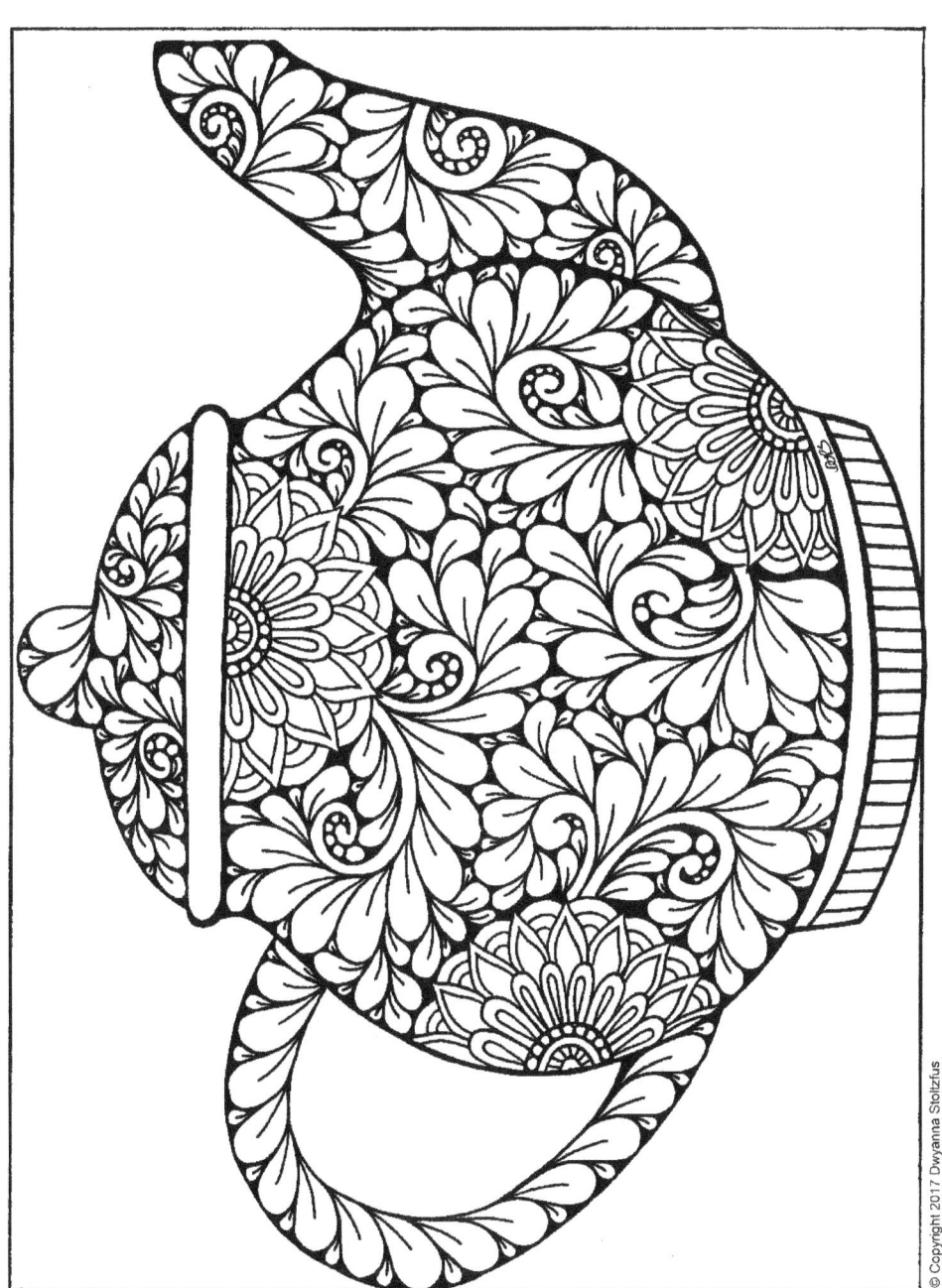

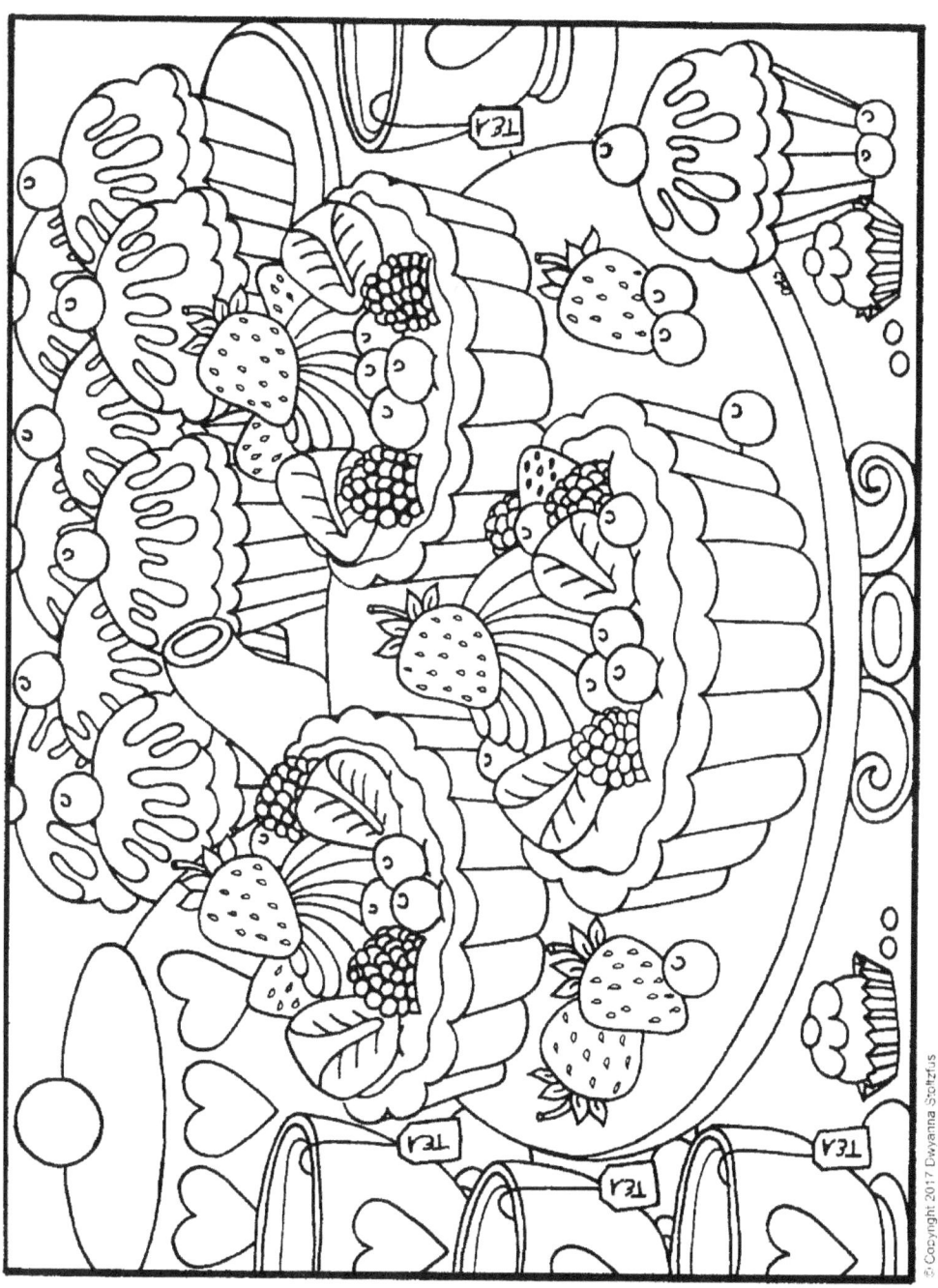

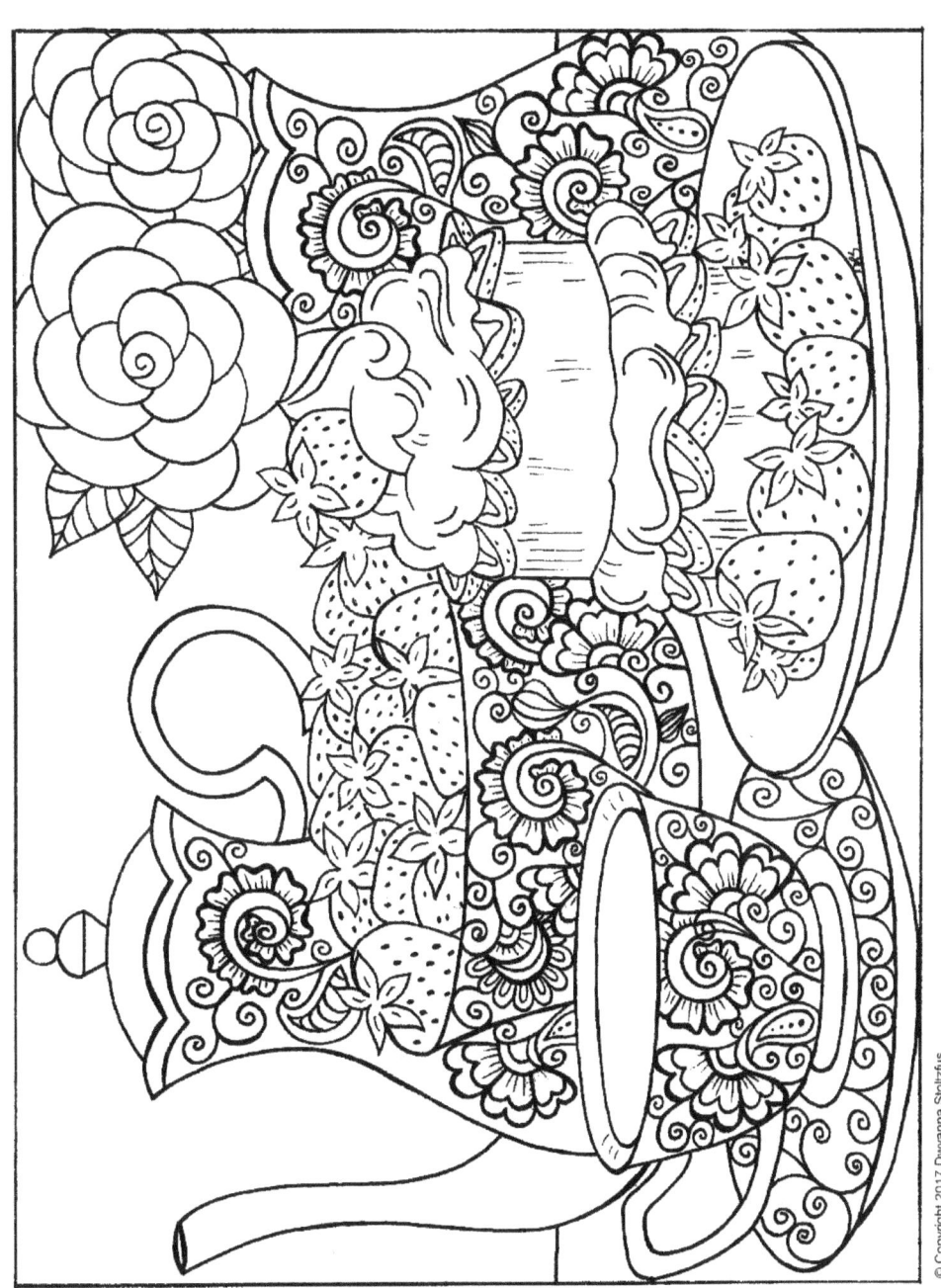

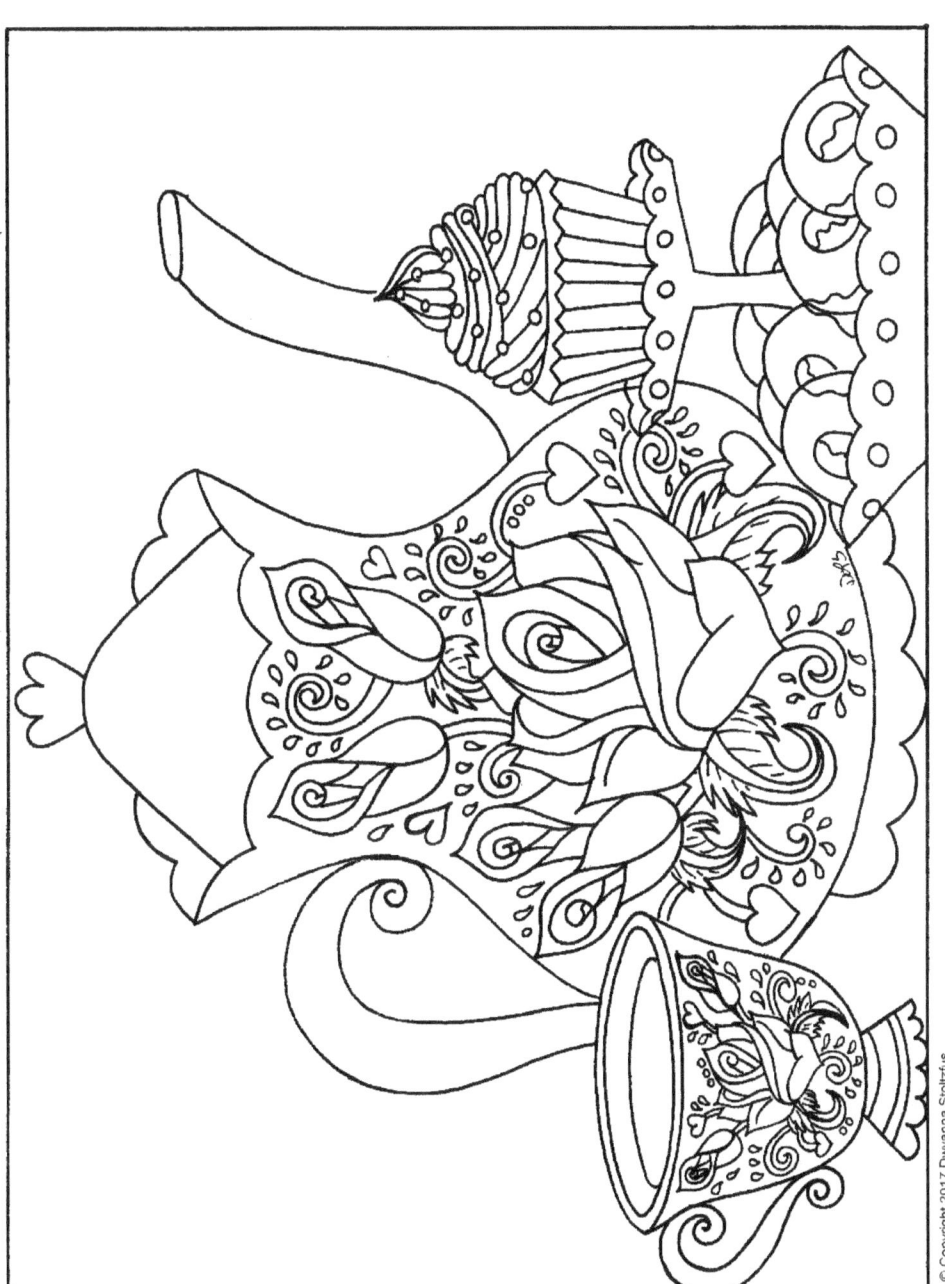

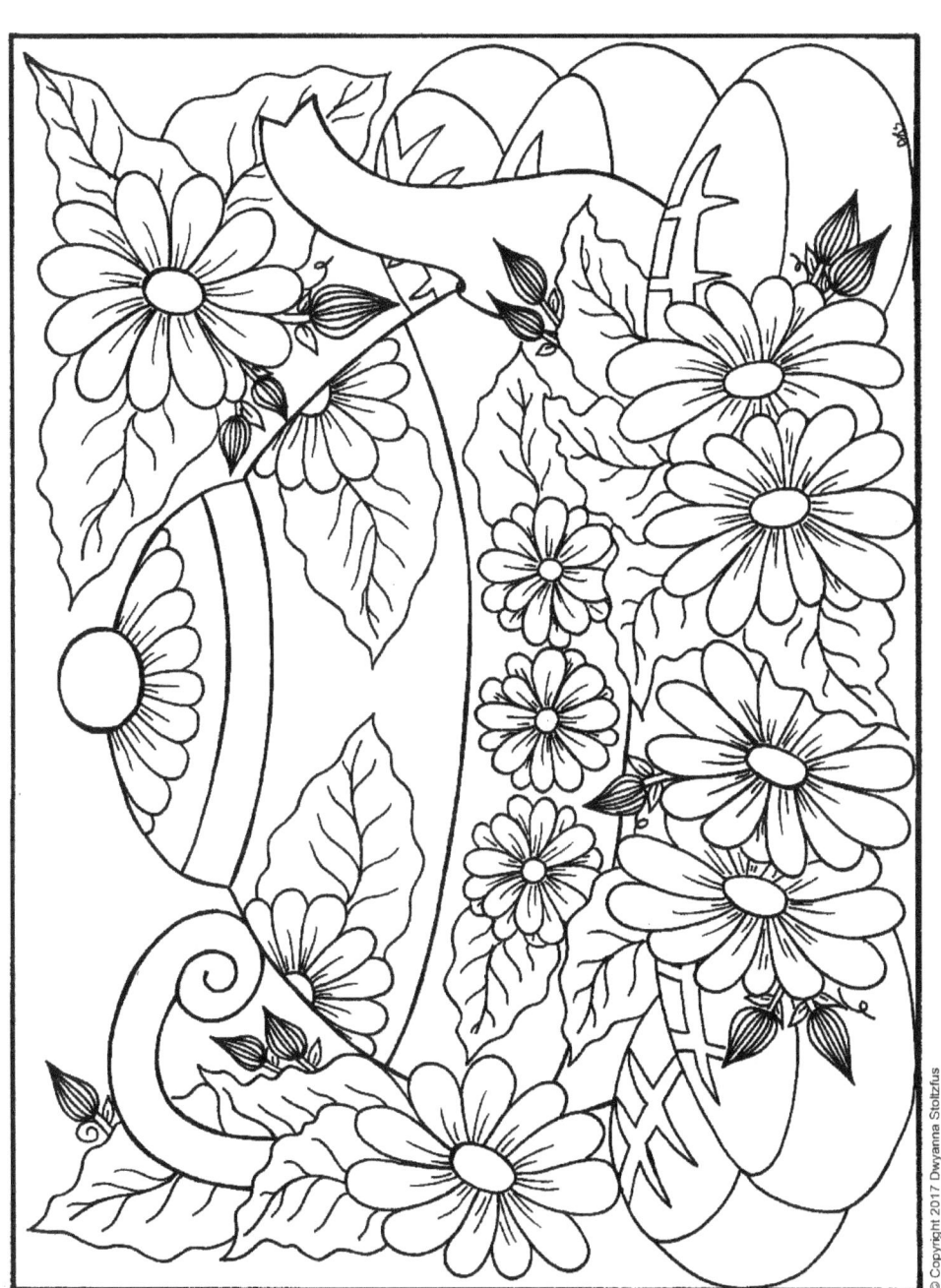

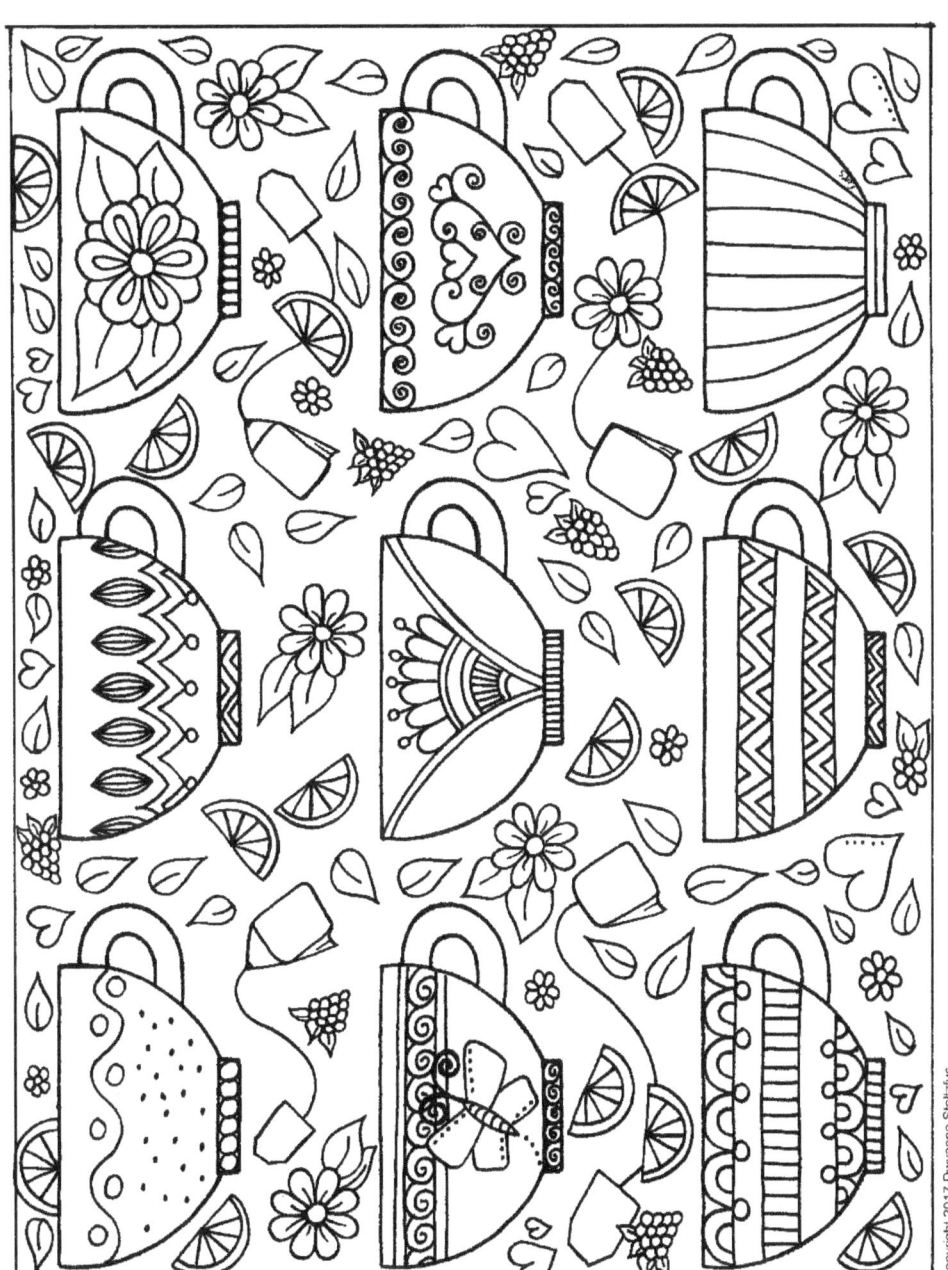

www.ingramcontent.com/pod-product-compliance
Lightning Source LLC
Chambersburg PA
CBHW070315230526
45470CB00002B/884